P9-AQJ-966

DISCARDED

# THE RADICAL LEFT IN THE HUNGARIAN REVOLUTION OF 1848

LASZLO DEME

EAST EUROPEAN QUARTERLY, BOULDER
DISTRIBUTED BY COLUMBIA UNIVERSITY PRESS
NEW YORK

1976

EAST EUROPEAN MONOGRAPHS, NO. XIX

---

Laszlo Deme is Professor of History
at New College, University of South Florida


Library of Congress Card Catalogue Number 76-3076
ISNB 0-914710-12-5

Printed in the United States of America

*To Elaine*

TABLE OF CONTENTS

TABLE OF CONTENTS

# INTRODUCTION

1848 was the year of revolutions in Europe, and Hungary, too, experienced a major political and social upheaval. Hungary had two basic questions to solve in that year. As a feudal country, she had to institute modern economic and social systems. As part of the multinational Habsburg Monarchy, Hungary wished to free herself from Austrian influence and at the same time had to cope with her own non-Magyar nationalities' political aspirations. Thus, the problems of social progress and of conflicting national desires required simultaneous solutions.

The struggle for national independence failed and the nationalities problem was unresolved in 1848 but by abolishing feudalism Hungary accomplished one of the most important changes in her thousand year old history. The revolution also placed Hungary in the main stream of world history. Alone among the peoples of Europe, the Magyars succeeded in taking a unified national stand in defense of their freedom. The revolutionary war against the Habsburg armies was on a larger scale and longer duration than elsewhere in Europe and also brought Russian troops for the first time to the Carpathian Basin.

This monograph will not attempt to give a detailed history of Hungary during the revolution. Its purpose is to examine the contribution to social progress and national freedom made by Hungarian radicals in 1848. The radicals were selected as the topic of this investigation because they, more than any other group, were responsible for the outbreak of the revolution and did the utmost to make it succeed.

The accomplishments of Hungarian radicalism were determined by the internal conditions of the country. Hungarian radicals, as radicals elsewhere in Europe, derived their ideology from the egalitarian tradition of the Great French Revolution. Therefore, despite Hungary's backwardness, the radicals asserted democratic principles and worked toward this goal during the revolution.

In 1848, the political spectrum in Hungary ranged from conservatives to liberals to, on the extreme left, radicals, a minority which wanted greater change than did the other groups. These three political groups are distinguishable by the solutions each offered to the essential questions of feudal social order and dependence of Hungary on Austria within the Habsburg Monarchy.

The conservatives affirmed their allegiance to the *Gesamtmonarchie* of the Habsburgs and to the government but did not believe in the feudal social order. In their 1847 program, they recommended, among other important reforms, that the settlement of feudal obligations be eased for the peasants. Even the conservatives recognized that the feudal system prevented Hungary's progress.

The liberals, who were the opposition until 1848, assumed power in April 1848. Among them were some of Hungary's most outstanding politicians: Count Lajos Batthyány, Lajos Kossuth and Ferenc Deák who became members of the first responsible cabinet. The liberals changed Hungary from a feudal monarchy whose nobility had retained all political rights and whose peasantry had carried all the burdens of the state to a liberal constitutional state. Through legislative action and due legal process, the peasants were liberated from serfdom. Civil liberties, equality before the law and the right to own land were granted to everyone. The King was to exercise executive power through a cabinet responsible to a popularly-elected parliament. The liberals reduced the relationship of Hungary to Austria to a "personal union": a common allegiance to the person of the monarch.

The new state created by Hungarian liberals represented great advances but Hungary was still behind France after her first constitution was instituted in 1791. The new legislation in Hungary did not refer to "active or passive" citizens but in fact followed that concept by granting universal civil liberties and limiting suffrage through property and income requirements. About half the adult male population was enfranchised: a proportionately fewer number than in France in 1791.

Remaining intact in Hungary the summer of 1848 were a hereditary upper house, titles of nobility, extensive ecclesiastic holdings and feudal remnants such as noble hunting rights.

Even greater change and progress was desired by a group of young intellectuals who organized a revolutionary demonstration on March 15, 1848 in Budapest and succeeded in taking over the administration of the capital for one month. At the head of these radical intellectuals stood Sándor Petőfi, the greatest Hungarian poet of that period; Mór Jókai, a famous romantic novelist; and Pál Vasvári, a young history teacher. These intellectuals formed one branch of Hungarian radicalism.

As events moved, the young intellectuals lost the chance to participate directly in the exercise of power. But, as a political force they were augmented by a number of important noble politicians with similar views who were deputies in the first representative Assembly. They formed another branch of Hungarian radicalism.

During the spring and summer of 1848, these two groups formulated the ideology of Hungarian radicalism and worked for its acceptance in the assembly, in the newspapers and on the streets of Budapest. The intellectuals were republicans. The radicals proposed universal suffrage and destruction of the rigid class barriers. They wished to complete the liberation of the peasantry by abolishing all vestiges of feudalism. They demanded the emancipation of the Jews and were, initially, more sympathetic than any other group of Magyars to the national aspirations of the non-Magyar nationalities in Hungary.

In some ways, the radicals strived to correct the shortcomings of Hungarian liberalism. But by proposing universal suffrage and a republican form of government, they raised problems which liberalism of the first half of the nineteenth century could not solve.

In their policy toward Austria the radicals clearly deviated from the liberals. At the end of the summer, the Habsburg Court, with a renewal of confidence, attempted to subordinate Hungary to Vienna again. The Batthyány Government tried to reach an accord with the Court on almost any terms. It remained to the radicals to oppose submission to Vienna and they even considered a second revolution to preserve the integrity of Hungary.

On the question of Hungarian national rights the radicals were in complete agreement with Lajos Kossuth, the most popular figure in the country. During September they established an alliance with Kossuth which led to armed resistance against the Imperial troops.

* * *

Parts of this study have been previously published. Analysis of the radicals' activities in March and April 1848 is partly based on the author's article "The Committee of Public Safety in the Hungarian Revolution of 1848" (*Canadian Slavic Studies*, Fall 1971). Similarly, the most important radical organization during the summer of 1848 was examined in an article entitled "The Society for Equality in the Hungarian Revolution of 1848" (*Slavic Review,* Spring 1972).

The author wishes to express his appreciation to Professor István Deák of Columbia University for reading the entire manuscript several times and providing much valuable advice. The assistance of Professor George Mayer in assuming part of the author's teaching responsibilities for a term at New College is also gratefully acknowledged. Above all the author would like to thank his wife, Elaine, for her encouragement and understanding during the preparation of this study and for the help she provided by editing and typing the manuscript.

Laszlo Deme

New College, University of South Florida
Sarasota, Florida

# CHAPTER ONE
# HUNGARY AND HER PLACE IN EUROPE

In 1848 Hungary was a kingdom of 125,600 square miles and was part of the Habsburg Monarchy. The Hungarians had come to the Carpathian Basin toward the end of the ninth century A.D. and after accepting Christianity and feudal institutions in the eleventh century under St. Stephen, Hungary became a member of the European state system.

During the Middle Ages, Hungary played a significant role in the political life of Europe and served as an important obstacle to Ottoman expansion during the second half of the fifteenth century.

The medieval prominence of the country ended with its crushing defeat by Suleiman the Magnificent at Mohács in 1526. King Louis II was killed and the nobility decimated. The central region of Hungary was occupied by the Turks for 150 years and the Crown of Hungary went to the House of Habsburg. This dynasty was to rule until 1918.

The Habsburgs eventually liberated the Turkish-occupied territories and reunited the country but the Hungarians were never completely happy with their rule. The Habsburgs, who were also Holy Roman Emperors, subordinated Hungarian national interests to those of the Empire. While in other European countries, rulers tended to serve the interests of their nationals along with those of their dynasty, Habsburg dynastic interests were not identical with those of Hungary.

This situation created antagonism between the nation and its ruling house. In the seventeenth century there were three major anti-Habsburg movements involving large-scale and prolonged warfare. Early in the eighteenth century an uprising led by the most influential Magyar noble of the time, Prince Ferenc Rákóczi, resulted in the dethronement of the Habsburgs and the election of Rákóczi as "ruling prince" by the Hungarian Diet. Rákóczi's uprising ended in failure once the fighting between the Imperial troops and those of Louis XIV ceased, releasing the Imperial forces against the Hungarians. The only result of armed opposition was the periodic renewal of royal promises, seldom kept, to respect Hungary's laws.

The subordination of Magyar to dynastic interests and the resulting repeated armed opposition left a deep mark on the public mind. The politically-conscious nobility considered those who kept alive the spirit of resistance to Vienna the only "good" patriots and this attitude was an important underlying current of Magyar political behavior.

Besides keeping national consciousness alive, this feeling compelled the Habsburgs to allow Hungary to retain most of her national institutions. The Habsburgs never succeeded in breaking the hold of the Hungarian nobility over internal administration. The nobles retained a system of self-government in the counties and control over the serfs essentially the same as they had had before the Crown went to the Habsburgs.

In the more advanced European countries where the estates lost their power to the king, the institution of the monarchy was instrumental in the building of the modern state. In Hungary this was not so. Magyar nobles could proudly say that they had prevented their country from being governed by foreigners. But they also prevented progressive measures which some rulers, like Joseph II, wanted to institute and they did not initiate any reforms themselves. Thus, conditions changed little through the centuries and Hungary was still a feudal state in the middle of the nineteenth century.

While the nobility controlled local administration by adhering to the feudal constitution, it had to relinquish control over the central government. During the Habsburg rule, there was a Hungarian Court Chancellery in Vienna, demonstrating Hungary's separateness. But the Hungarian Chancellor was appointed for his loyalty to the ruling house and was responsible to the monarch alone. The Chancellor and his associates could not be regarded as an independent Hungarian government, and in practice were the instrument of the central Viennese War Council, Foreign Office and Treasury, which exercised control over all Habsburg territories.

The administration of military, financial and foreign affairs had been among the royal prerogatives since medieval times, and the Hungarian nobility had no legal basis to contest this arrangement. Hungary was the largest possession of the ruling house and, after the loss of Germany, the Habsburgs needed Hungary to maintain their status as a great power. The Hungarian Diet kept the power of the purse and control over recruitment to the King's army. Therefore, in order to receive revenues and soldiers from Hungary, the Habsburgs could not entirely ignore the country's wishes.

### A. *The State of Society in the First Decades of the Nineteenth Century.*

Hungary was a multi-national state. On the basis of language, the population in the middle of the nineteenth century was divided into the following groups:[1]

| | |
|---|---|
| Magyars | 5,413,327 |
| Rumanians | 2,477,611 |
| Slovaks | 1,842,320 |
| Croats | 1,263,908 |
| Germans | 1,247,122 |
| Serbians | 1,054,416 |
| Ruthenians | 478,310 |
| Saxons | 250,000 |
| Slovenians | 49,600 |
| Others (Bulgarians, Italians, Armenians, Gypsies and Jews) | 476,957 |
| Total | 14,553,571 |

The strongest among these groups were the Magyars but the figures indicate that they were only about 37 percent of the total population.[2] Among the non-Magyar nationalities, the Croats enjoyed a privileged position dating back to the twelfth century when their Kingdom had joined Hungary. They were governed by a viceroy (*ban*) and had a separate diet which was autonomous in local affairs. Transylvania also had a separate administration and diet established during the Turkish conquest and retained by the Habsburgs.

Socially, Hungary was a country of king, nobles and serfs, with the serfs owing feudal obligations to the nobles. Among these obligations, forced labor on the lands of the nobles, the so-called *robot*, was the most burdensome. The nobility constituted about 5 percent of the population and directly controlled about 70 percent of the arable land; the remainder was in the hands of the peasants.[3]

Among the nobility there was considerable stratification. A few hundred families, those with the titles of prince, count and baron, belonged to the high aristocracy and owned large estates varying from a few thousand to hundreds of thousands of acres. The others were referred to by the contradictory term of "common nobility" *(köznemesség)* or gentry. The gentry owned less land, lived closer to the people and was more patriotic than the high aristocracy, which often owed its titles and lands to the Habsburgs.

The difference between the aristocracy and gentry was expressed in the Diet. All members of the aristocracy had the right to sit in the Upper House, while the gentry elected two delegates from each county to the

Lower House. Only token representation was given to the cities and no representation at all was given to the *misera plebs contribuens*--the peasantry.

Hungary was virtually unaffected by the industrial revolution. In 1846 only 334,153 persons were engaged in a form of industry. Most of these were artisans and of this number only 23,400 worked in factories. There were only 21,512 merchants.[4]

Despite Hungary's backwardness, the great events of European history did not go by without consequence. The French Revolution of 1789 aroused great enthusiasm among a small group of intellectuals. The Napoleonic Wars created new markets for the country's agricultural products and, as everywhere in Europe, grain prices rose and estate owners attempted to increase their output to meet the new demand.

After the wars, the new demand for wool also brought changes. Production for foreign markets introduced new elements in the nobility's thinking and also led to a crisis in agricultural production. Under feudal conditions, the larger estates could not increase production and improve the quality of their goods efficiently. The forced labor of the serfs was of low quality. Landowners lacked capital to invest and could not get enough credit for expansion. There were no banks, no railroads, no modern shipping, hardly any industry.[5] If the country wanted to modernize, it had to make significant adjustments.

B. *The Era of Reform: Széchenyi and Kossuth.*

The crisis of feudalism was first recognized by Count István Széchenyi, a large landowner. After extensive travels in Western Europe, Széchenyi published several works in which he suggested how Hungary could overcome her problems. In *Credit (Hitel)* he cited the lack of credit as the most urgent problem of the landed nobility and recommended the establishment of a national bank. Conditions would also improve, he believed, if the system of entail would be abolished, allowing the free transfer of title to land. He stressed the need for the development of the country's meager transportation system and the establishment of industrial enterprises. He was the first among his compatriots to state the simple truth that free men work better and he advocated the abolition of serfdom through friendly agreements between landlords and serfs.

Széchenyi clearly stood for the modernization of Hungary. However, he envisaged this change occurring under the Habsburgs with the relationship with Austria left intact. Also, he hoped this transformation would take place under the leadership of the aristocracy.

*Credit,* and Széchenyi's other works, *Light* (*Világ,* 1831), and

*Stadium* (*State of Affairs,* 1833), caused a great sensation and convinced an educated segment of the nobility of the need for change. Széchenyi is regarded as the greatest reformer of nineteenth century Hungary and cannot be considered a revolutionary.

Lajos Kossuth, a member of the gentry, offered the country another program of modernization. He became known in the 1830's as a politician of the opposition and an outstanding journalist. He was imprisoned by the Metternich government between 1837-40. After his release, he became editor of the largest newspaper and influenced public opinion in Hungary more than anyone else.

Kossuth was in agreement with many of Széchenyi's ideas. He also wished serfdom abolished. Kossuth urged, though, that ties with Austria be loosened and that Hungary achieve economic and political independence within the framework of the monarchy. This viewpoint found ready acceptance and popularity with the politically conscious in Hungary.

Kossuth believed that protective tariffs were necessary to prevent competition from more highly-industrialized Austria and to promote nascent industries. He stressed the importance of a railroad system as a step towards independence from Vienna and he proposed that Budapest be connected with Fiume, Hungary's only seaport, and a maritime trade increased with other countries.

Kossuth wished political, social and economic changes to be carried out by or with the help of the gentry, to which he belonged, rather than under the aristocracy's leadership.

Thus, Hungarians were offered two programs for the country's improvement. Since these programs differed in essential features, a sharp controversy arose between the two men. Kossuth was attacked for his anti-Austrian activities and accused of preparing a revolution which, Széchenyi thought, would be disastrous. Kossuth denied his charges and continued pressing for his program.[6]

Both men were opposed by the majority of the aristocracy, a considerable segment of the gentry and the government. Their arguments, however, contributed to the crystalization of the currents of political thought.

C. *Political Reform in the 1830's and 1840's.*

The most important battles between the conservatives and liberals took place in the Lower House of the Diet where the representatives of the gentry sat. The period of reform started at the 1825-27 Diet; the first meeting of the estates since 1812. Against the absolutist tendencies of the Metternich government, this Diet reasserted earlier legislation of

1790-91. The Diet affirmed that Hungary was a "free country," i.e., "not dependent upon any other country, having its own constitution, governed by her legally-crowned king according to her own laws and customs and not on the pattern of other [Habsburg] provinces.[7]

This legislation was a restatement of the old liberties often violated, and can be regarded as the point of departure for the reform peroid initiated by Széchenyi. He was instrumental in the establishment of the Hungarian Academy of Sciences which had the primary responsibility for the cultivation of the Hungarian language. This was badly needed in a country whose official language was Latin.

With the founding of the Academy, attention was focused on the language problem which became a central issue at following Diets. For the Magyars, the replacement of Latin with Hungarian was a question of progress. The same men who fought for the abolition of serfdom also took a stand for the use of the Hungarian language. In 1844 Hungarian became the official language of the country to be used in the legislature courts, schools and the administrative apparatus of the state.[8] To the non-Magyar nationalities, replacing Latin with Hungarian was not progress but, rather, a manifestation of Magyar nationalism and they considered it a threat to their own languages. Only the Croats were allowed to use their language in their diet and administration, but, still, their national pride was injured by being forced to communicate with the Hungarian Diet in Hungarian.

While liberalism and nationalism mutually supported each other in other European countries and represented a unifying force in society, in a multi-national state like Hungary, they led to division along nationality lines.

The second significant topic argued at every session of the Diet was the extension of the rights of the peasantry and the abolition of the feudal economic and political order. The liberals demanded civil liberties and property rights be granted to all. Under their pressure, the Diet which met from 1832-36 allowed for the conversion of feudal obligations into monetary units to be paid annually.[9] The 1839-40 Diet made a permanent monetary settlement possible if both parties agreed and the peasant could make the prescribed payment.[10]

In 1836 the Diet decided to tax the poorest nobles who were living and working on a peasant lot. This was a departure from the ancient principle of tax exemption for nobles and can be regarded as the first step toward civil equality. At the same time the Diet allowed the villages to elect local officials.

In the 1843-44 meeting, the estates accepted the principle of equality of taxation, the abolition of the tithe and the right of commoners to own property.[11] It was a long way from decisions of "principles" to realities, still, these actions precipitated the final disappearance of the feudal system.

The regularity of the Diet's sessions, Kossuth's persistent calls for reform and the increasing number of newspapers created a lively political atmosphere necesitating the formulation of party programs. Typical of this period, even the conservatives presented themselves as progressives in their 1846 platform. The platform had a long list of reforms to be ". . .enacted in accordance with conservative principles" and pledged to support the government against the opposition. The conservatives proposed to guarantee freedom of opinion, to facilitate the settlement of feudal obligations, and to improve the criminal code, prison conditions and public administration.[12]

The program of the liberal opposition was more specific. On the basis of Kossuth's draft, Ferenc Deák formulated the "Declaration of the Opposition" in 1847.[13] Calling themselves the "constitutional opposition," the liberals claimed the right to supervise the government with the government responsible to the parliamentary majority. They proposed that "everyone should share in the public burden," (taxation), and that commoners, particularly those in the cities, should be granted civil rights. Most important, they demanded that the feudal obligations be abolished and the nobility compensated for its resulting losses. In addition, they urged freedom of assembly and the press, circumscribed by appropriate laws, and they desired union with Transylvania.

The liberals even gave advice on how to reorganize the Austrian provinces of the Habsburgs. They stated that greater harmony and identity of interest would prevail in the whole Monarchy if the Austrian hereditary provinces would be granted constitutions in accordance with the principles of justice and the demands of the age.

Thus, Hungary approached the year of revolutions in an atmosphere of liberal reforms to which a significant part of her nobility was committed.

# CHAPTER II

## THE BACKGROUND OF HUNGARIAN RADICALISM

### A. *The Martinovics Conspiracy.*

Although in Hungary of the 1840's progressive elements were still struggling to emancipate the serfs, radicalism did have some tradition. In the 1790's the ideas of French Revolution were received as enthusiastically by some Hungarian intellectuals as in Germany and other parts of Europe. Their sympathy for *liberté, égalité* and *fraternité* took the form of a Jacobin conspiracy in 1794 led by a priest, Ignác Martinovics.

Martinovics, (1755-95), had such varied careers as army chaplain, professor of physics at the University of Lemberg (Lvov) and informer for the Habsburg secret police.[1] In the spring of 1794, he formed two secret societies: the "Secret Society of Reformers" for the nobility and the "Society for Liberty and Equality" for the others.

In both the "Cathechisms" Martinovics wrote for each society, he advocated the overthrow of the monarchy and the proclamation of a republic. In the catechism for the nobles, he stressed their political grievances against Austria and benefits to be derived from doing away with the king, high clergy and high aristocracy. He promised that after the liberation only the nobility could own property and the commoners would have to rent the land from them.[2] This last statement was absent from the commoners' catechism. Here the lack of distinction between noble and commoner was emphasized. Serfdom was termed slavery and the sovereignty of the people was proclaimed.[3]

Martinovics' plans were vague but he still recruited prominent writers, poets, lawyers and civil servants to join his movement[4] who were led to believe that the French Convent would come to their aid. The conspiracy was discovered in July 1794 and at the ensuing trial, 53 members were accused of high treason. Seven of them including Martinovics, were executed and the others received long prison sentences. No voices of dissatisfaction were heard in Hungary for the next 30 years.

The Martinovics conspiracy was a feeble attempt on the part of a few isolated individuals to create a republic. Martinovics sensed correctly that republicanism would appeal to two potentially radical groups:

idealistic noblemen with modest estates and plebian intellectuals. The events of 1848 bear this out: both the idealistic nobleman and the plebian intellectual were typical of the radicals in that year and formed the left wing in the 1848-49 revolution.

B. *The Two Branches of Radicalism: County Nobles and Young Hungary.*

In the pre-March 1848 period, any republican in East Central Europe was a radical. In this sense, some of the gentry were radicals. József Madarász, a future radical deputy, was one such "leftist" nobleman. Already in the 1830's he discussed the possibilities of the republican form of government with his friends.[5] They must have been generally known for their republicanism because when introduced to Ferenc Deák, a leader of the liberal opposition, Deák greeted them with, "Well, you revolutionaries, how are you?"[6]

Madarász and his young friends were not alone. Others, in the solitude of their country estates, were studying political systems and coming to similar conclusions. Bertalan Szemere, the future Minister of the Interior in the revolutionary Cabinet, wrote in the early 1840's that the republican form of government was the ". . .only road to salvation for Hungary."[7] Mór Perczel, a prominent general in the revolutionary war, wrote in his memoirs that he and his friends ". . .derived their political philosophy from the history of the French Revolution."[8]

Young men who came to Budapest to become university students, journalists, lawyers, writers and poets were known as "Young Hungary" and became the vanguard of the 1848 revolution.

In general, these youth did not win seats in the Assembly nor became military leaders, but they organized and led street demonstrations, wrote the radical newspapers and created the revolutionary atmosphere. These men represented radicalism most consistently and became the "extreme left" in 1848.

C. *The Ideology of Young Hungary before 1848.*

Metternich became aware of the existence of "Young Hungary" by 1837, and he considered it dangerous to the security of the state.[9] By the mid-forties, the views of a sizable group among the young literati in Budapest differed fundamentally not only from those of Metternich but even from those of the Hungarian Opposition.

These men, mostly in their twenties, included the greatest Hungarian poet of the nineteenth century, Sándor Petőfi; his close friend and Hungary's most popular novelist, Mór Jókai; the well-read historian, Pál Vasvári; and the brilliant journalists József Irinyi and Albert Pálffy. There were numerous other writers, poets, journalists and university students who were to form the radical left in 1848. This group was not large, yet it exercised greater influence than its numbers would indicate through its journals and newspapers.

The culture and spirit of change that emanated from France was the greatest single influence upon these men. Jókai wrote in his memoirs:

> "We were all Frenchmen. We read only Lamartine, Michelet, Louis Blanc, Sue, Victor Hugo and Béranger. If we deigned to read an English or German poet, it was Shelley or Heine, disowned by their own countrymen and English or German with respect only to their language: in spirit, they were French. In Perőfi's case, the adoration of the French was a real cult. His room was filled with valuable engravings of the men of the '89 revolution which he had had brought from Paris. They represented Robespierre, St. Just, Marat and Madame Roland."[10]

Elsewhere, Jókai admits loving Scott's *Ivanhoe*, Dickens and Cooper, and he wrote that he "went into a daze" upon reading "King Lear."[11] His remarks indicate the main trend and are supported by the statements of others. József Irinyi wrote in his travel notes about France in 1846:

> "I esteem the French nation very highly. Of all foreign nations, I love the French the most and demand the most from them. They have glorified humanity and have done more for the cause of liberty and for the elucidation of principles and ideas than any other nation. For these reasons, I agree with Heine who says: 'Liberty is the new religion of our age. . . . The chosen people of this new religion are the French. They have written the first gospels of this new religion. Paris is the new Jerusalem and the Rhine is the River Jordan."[12]

The adoration of France was coupled with a great interest in history, and the young intellectuals looked to the past for justification of their progressive ideas. Petőfi referred to a history of wars for freedom as his "prayer book."[13] Vasvári, a student of history, believed that happiness was the ultimate goal of mankind and it was difficult to attain not because of nature, but because of the ill will of some individuals impeding the progress of the "world spirit." For Vasvári, everything that occurs in the world has only one purpose: the enlightenment of humanity.[14] He found the Middle Ages a period of dark barbarism and ignorance and agreed with Voltaire that prior to the eighteenth century the source of backwardness and stagnation was the people's lack of education.[15]

Although the young intellectuals hardly mention Hegel's name, to some degree they were all under his influence. The guiding force of history, according to Vasvári and his friends, was the world spirit. He wrote that "man rules over nature and the world spirit rules over man. The principles and the ideas of his age govern the deeds of man."[16]

In the progress of history, the world spirit expresses itself through great men, but Vasvári's great men were not the same as those of Hegel. For Vasvári, men "in whose hearts the profound ideas for the happiness of mankind were born and who did magnificent deeds for world freedom and the happiness of humanity [were great]. . . . Franklin and Washington are more highly regarded in the eyes of the world than Napoleon and Julius Caesar."[17]

Vasvári considered Michelet's writings as ideal works of history. Responding to German critics, he defended Michelet's method as stimulating, inspiring and bringing history close to the students. He warned against "looking at the intellectual capital of the world through Berlin or Leipzig eyeglasses" and declared the Hungarian national character to be closest to that of the French. He selected France as an excellent model for Hungary's intellectual development.[18]

The ideas of world freedom, anti-monarchism and progress inspired Petőfi in his poetry. A poem written (but not published), in 1844 entitled "Against the Kings" says that kings were only needed as long as the people were children and had to play. The fate of Louis XVI of France was the first bolt of lightening which wrote in the sky with the blood of kings that the world was no longer in its childhood.[19]

Hatred for monarchy went together with love of freedom and the desire to fight for it. In a poem written in 1846, Petőfi described his vision of a battlefield where, under red flags, enslaved nations would take a stand against tyranny and he wrote that this was where he wanted to give his life for the sacred cause.[20]

Enthusiasm for the abstract notion of "world freedom"was accompanied by criticism of the aristocracy, especially the gentry. In a letter to a fellow poet, Petőfi defined his program as follows:

> ". . . folklore is the real poetry. We should make it predominate! If the people are the master in poetry, they will be closer to mastering politics also. This is the task of our century. This is the aim of every noble heart which has seen too much of the martyrdom of millions to secure the leisure and pleasure of a few thousand. To heaven with the people! To hell with the artistocracy!"[21]

Petőfi's exhortation referred not only to the content of poetry but also to its artistic form. Much of his work was written in the style of songs of the peasantry with whom he often identified. Indeed, his works served as models for the folkloristic style which prevailed in Hungarian poetry for the remainder of the century.

Petőfi believed that the leader of a sixteenth century peasant war, György Dózsa, was the "most glorious man in Hungarian history." He hoped that some day a statue would be erected to the peasant leader and ". . .perhaps, mine will be next to it," he wrote.[22]

Both Petőfi and Vasvári shared the intense feelings of anticlericalism with many revolutionaries. Vasvári's anticlericalism arose from his denial of the existence of God. In explaining the origins of religion, he wrote that primitive man, not understanding natural phenomena such as thunder and lightening, began to worship them.[23]

Petőfi's concerns were more pragmatic. He disliked the clergy because it was reactionary.

"They are the children of the night, therefore, you see them everywhere fighting against the sunshine of freedom."

Petőfi hoped that the clergy would be ultimately destroyed, bringing progress, freedom and happiness. He also believed that mankind had to continue its struggle until "everyone can take an equal share from the basket of plenty" and had the same rights.[25]

Vasvári went further and dreamed of a "perfect republic" in which the "cruel aristocracy of wealth" would disappear and the people would toil for themselves. All heavy work would be done by machines and not only the slaves would be liberated from the yoke but also the beasts of burden.[26]

Having expressed such sentiments, it is not suprising that it was Vasvári who attempted to explain Cabet's utopian socialism to the workers is Budapest in 1848.

***

Although not a member of the intellectual circle of Young Hungary, the colorful figure of Mihály Táncsics deserves mention. He had personally experienced the misery of serfdom; he became a weaver, later an elementary school teacher and he even traveled on foot all over Europe. He became known in Hungary as the author of numerous pamphlets and books.

Táncsics, along with many others, demanded the abolition of censorship and equality of rights. More vehemently than anyone else, he demanded social justice for the peasantry. He reiterated the theme that the peasants were the most important class because the country was sustained through their labor and taxation.[27] He called for the liberation of the serfs without compensation,[28] unprecedented in his time: "This land is ours; we cultivate it and if [i.e., the nobility] do not want to declare this truth by law, we will proclaim it ourselves!"[29]

It is small wonder that he was accused of haranguing the peasantry against the established order and was imprisoned in Buda. His liberation was one of the first acts of the victorious revolutionaries on March 15.

Young Hungary reflected much of the culture of its time. Indeed, these men were "all French" in their orientation. They followed the most progressive tradition in Europe. Long before they could act, they had dethroned the old gods. Stemming from their readings from the French enlightenment, they glorified reason and coupled this with wild enthusiasm for romanticism and its new gods of freedom and progress. In final analysis, they believed in the perfectability of mankind. In this respect they were true revolutionaries.

Were they also original thinkers? Only in small part. Young Hungary did not create the ideas they followed but they were, perhaps, the only ones in Hungary to understand that the country had to undergo a transformation similar to that of France following the revolution of 1789. They recognized the need for a sharp break with the feudal past. Before any of the leading policticians, Young Hungary realized freedom could not be attained without fighting for it on the battlefield.

## CHAPTER III

## THE RADICAL LEFT IN ACTION: THE MAKING OF THE REVOLUTION

### A. *The Last Days of the Old Regime.*

Many Hungarians approached 1848 with great expectation. From the "progressive conservatives" to the republican radicals, everyone desired some kind of change. The conservatives emphasized gradualism; Kossuth and the constitutional opposition urged speedy reform. Only the radicals wanted revolution.

From November 12, 1847 on, the Diet remained in session in Pozsony[1] and debated continuously about reforms. The principal figure of the Opposition in the Lower House was Lajos Kossuth; in the Upper House it was Count Lajos Batthyány. The Opposition held about one half of the seats in the Lower House, the remainder was in the hands of the conservatives who supported the government. The radicals were not represented at all.[2]

Until the end of February 1848 there were no indications that this was to be the last meeting of the estates in Hungarian history. Following the pattern of the early 1840's, under liberal pressure, the Diet made slow progress toward the abolition of feudalism. Prior to February 1848, the Lower House agreed to tax part of the nobility; it made the final redemption of serfs obligatory in those villages where the majority desired it; and it abolished the entail. These were decisions of "principle" only, however, and the formulation of the actual laws was pending in joint committees of Upper and Lower Houses.[3] The situation became even more complicated when signs of disintergration appeared in the Opposition and there was talk about forming a "center" party around Széchenyi.[4]

While these developments were taking place in Pozsony, nothing unusual was happening in Budapest. Liberal nobles met in their club, the Opposition Circle, and talked. The young radicals habitually met in their favorite café, the Pilvax, and also talked. There was no organization of any kind yet.

According to one of the participants, Albert Nyári, a group was formed among university students in Budapest in early December 1847. At first, they met in a newspaper office and discussed current political questions. Vasvári was an active member. When attendance greatly increased, they moved to the Pilvax which was also the meeting place of Petőfi, Jókai and other young writers. Nyári described the coffee house as follows:

"If you entered this coffee house in the evening, you would have thought you were in a parliament. The intelligent young men, sitting at long tables, were discussing world events. Newspapers were read aloud and the young men were surrounded by hundreds of others. The coffee house became a temple of freedom, where inspired youth came to sacrifice to the god of freedom."[6]

Although the young radicals had no formal organization prior to March 1848, at least they had a forum where they were heard by "hundreds of others."

B. *The Effects of the February Revolution in Paris.*

1. *Pozsony: Revolutionary change through the Diet and King.*

On March 3, six days late, the news arrived in Pozsony that demonstrators in Paris had captured the Hotel de Ville and the Tuilleries and the monarchy had collapsed with the abdication of Louis Philippe. Kossuth seized the opportunity and the same day, amid great excitement in the Diet, he delivered a historic speech to the Lower House.[7]

Analyzing the conditions in the Habsbury Monarchy, Kossuth called for thorough reform. He condemned the absolutist-bureaucratic setup in Austria and suggested that a constitutional structure be established with respect for each nationality which would bring real and lasting unity.

Kossuth demanded fundamental changes but remained a loyal subject of the Habsburgs. He emphasized that change was beneficial not only for the people but would also glorify the dynasty. He stressed that in the future the magnificent throne of the Habsburgs should derive its strength from liberty.

To solve Hungary's problems, Kossuth called for an Address to the Throne from both Houses communicating the following decisions: equality of taxation; abolition of serfdom with compensation to the nobles; granting of "political rights" and the establishment of a government responsible to the parliamentary majority. The Address was to state explicitly that the government should be "independent, national and free from any foreign interference."

In short, Kossuth demanded far-reaching reforms which implied drastic transformation of Hungary as well as of the Habsburg Empire. At this moment, Kossuth seemed to hope for a "revolution" from above: change accomplished through the established authorities, Diet and King.

Kossuth's speech had repercussions in both Hungary and abroad. It was enthusiastically received in Vienna and was a factor in the outbreak of the revolution there on March 13.[8] The Lower House responded by immediately accepting his proposals. The Upper House, however, was not in session and so could not discuss nor act upon his recommendations. Those with the authority to convene the Upper House, the Palatine Archduke Stephen and a few others, were in Vienna receiving instructions. Without the approval of the Upper House, the proposal could not be sent officially to the King.

Kossuth realized that considerable opposition could be expected from Vienna official circles and the small but powerful and wealthy Hungarian high aristocracy. He was not even sure of the reaction of the conservative element in the gentry. A contemporary noted that Kossuth considered his fellow deputies "incredibly timid" and so he decided to use the pressure of public opinion. He gave his approval to the so-called Opposition Circle in Budapest to organize popular support by circulating a petition making the same demands he had asked for in the Diet.[9]

To give greater weight to the petition, the Opposition Circle decided to organize a popular demonstration on March 19, a "banquet" in the French tradition. The planned meeting and the petition were extremely important because the public was provided with the means to participate in the nation's political life and marked the emergence of two centers of action: the Diet in Pozsony and the radical Budapest.

2. *Budapest: Revolutionary change through popular action.*

In Budapest, the proposed banquet gained attention before March 15 and the petition formulated by a young radical journalist, József Irinyi, became known as the Twelve Points.[10] Since the first events of the revolution centered around the Twelve Points, it is appropriate to quote them in full:

WHAT DOES THE HUNGARIAN NATION WISH? THAT THERE SHOULD BE PEACE, FREEDOM AND CONCORD

1. We wish the freedom of the press and the abolition of censorship
2. Responsible government in Budapest.
3. Annual meetings of the parliament in Pest. *(sic)*
4. Equality before the law in civil and religious matters.
5. A national guard.
6. Equality of taxation.
7. Abolition of the feudal burdens.
8. Jury system on the basis of representation and equality.
9. A national bank.

10. The armed forces should swear allegiance to the constitution; our Hungarian soldiers should not be sent abroad; foreign soldiers should be removed from our soil.
11. Political prisoners of state should be freed.
12. Union with Transylvania.

Equality, Liberty, Fraternity!"[11]

The Twelve Points undoubtedly responded to the national and social needs of Hungary. For this very reason, some of them voiced aspirations of national independence and others pointed to social reform.

Yet, of the twelve demands only four dealt with national issues, (No. 2, Responsible Hungarian government; No. 9, National bank (financial independence from Austria); No. 10, Removal of foreign troops; and No. 12, Union with Transylvania). Even two of these combined social and national items. In No. 2 the responsibility of the government is just as important as its Hungarian charcter. No. 10 demanded the removal of foreign soldiers and the return of Hungarian soldiers who would swear allegiance not to the King but to the Constitution.

The remaining eight points dealt with social reform. Some of the demands showed continuity with the platform of the liberal opposition. They included everything the Opposition Program of 1847 had demanded and even more. The Twelve Points did not ask that "everyone share in the public burdens" or that the "commoners, especially in the cities be endowed with rights." "Equality of taxation" or "Equality before the law" are called for—obviously more emphatic and direct than were the previous demands.

Some of the Twelve Points went beyond reform and were openly revolutionary in character. No one in Hungary before March 1848 had publicly demanded that the armed forces should swear allegiance to the constitution instead of to the supreme war lord, the King. The liberation of political prisoners directly echoes Paris of 1789, not to mention the slogan of liberty, equality and fraternity. Thus, the Twelve Points were a synthesis of the progressive Hungarian national tradition and the revolutionary tradition of the continent, most notably France.

It is true that what we call "progressive national tradition" (such as manifested in the demands of the Opposition for the abolition of censorship, equality, etc.), also had its roots in the great French Revolution, which provided inspiration to all progressive movements of the century. This perhaps helps to explain why the Twelve Points resemble demands made elsewhere in Europe during those days.

In addition to the common source of inspiration, the similar oppressive conditions are other factors to be considered. In Vienna the first point of the university students' petition also was abolition of censorship along with freedom of teaching, religious equality and universal representation.[12] Young men in the Habsburg Monarchy, as well as on the larger European scene, reacted in a similar manner against the Metternich system.

The Twelve Points were discussed several times by the Opposition Circle between March 12-14.[13] Instead of sending them to the King or the Diet at once, it was decided that first hundreds of thousands of approving signatures would be collected throughout the country.[14] Thus, it looked as if nothing would transpire for some time to come. But on the evening of March 14 word came of the Viennese revolution of March 13 causing great excitement in Budapest. There could not have been more sensational news than that of the defeat of absolutism and Metternich's fall. It also seems to have propelled the Pilvax group into action.

The next day, March 15, Petőfi, Jókai, Vasvári and a fourth young revolutionary named Bulyovszky met at dawn and made plans for a popular demonstration demanding freedom of the press. This was the first of the Twelve Points and would eliminate what was to them the most hated aspect of the old system. Petőfi wrote, "Logically, the first step and duty of the revolution is to make the press free. . .that we will do! The rest I will entrust to God and to those destined to continue what was begun; I am destined only to give the first push."[15]

From Petőfi's apartment the four organizers went to the Pilvax and joined a crowd. An eyewitness described the scene of a great mass gathering in front of the café, cheering liberty. "Inside the café [there was] great turbulance, excited talk and violent outbursts."[16] Jókai read the Twelve Points which were greeted enthusiastically and Petőfi recited the "National Song"[17] which he had written two days earlier.

Rarely did a poem influence outcome of historic events as did this one. It called on Hungarians to stand up and shake off the chains of tryanny. It recalled their forefathers who had lived and died as free men, and urged the audience to do likewise: "Should we be slaves or free? This is the question. Choose!" The answer was unequivocal: "We swear by the God of Hungarians, we swear, we shall not be slaves anymore!"

After listening to Petőfi's poem, the young men started to march. Led by Petőfi, Jókai and Vasvári, they went to the university and, disrupting the lectures, they urged the students to accompany them. As the demonstration continued, the crowd grew larger as ordinary citizens of Pest, in spite of a steady downpour, joined with them.

At Petőfi's suggestion, the crowd proceeded from the University to a well-known printing shop nearby, where they planned to have the

Twelve Points and Petőfi's "National Song" printed without the censor's permission. An elected committee entered the shop and asked the owner, Landerer, to print the two manuscripts. A member of the committee described what happened:

> "Landerer said dryly, 'It is impossible, the permission is not on them.' We looked at each other and did not know what to do. Landerer whispered, 'seize one of the printing presses!' József Irinyi laid his hand on the biggest machine with these words: 'We seize this printing press in the name of the people!' 'I cannot resist force.' answered Landerer. With this, the workers burst out: 'Long live the people!'"[18]

While the poem and the Twelve Points were being quickly printed, Vasvári and Jókai delivered fervent speeches to the waiting crowd. The audience listened, huddled under open umbrellas and, when Jókai warned them that in an hour bullets might fall instead of rain, they all closed their umbrellas.[19]

As the first copy rolled off the press, one of the young men grabbed it, ran outside and raising it high shouted: "Here is the first child of the free press!"[20] Then Petőfi again recited his poem. The leaflets with the Twelve Points and the "Nationl Song" were distributed by the thousands and the crowd awaited the second act of the drama.

Petőfi and his friends called for a popular meeting at 3:00 p.m. that day. In spite of the continuing rain, about ten thousand persons gathered in front of the neo-classic columns of the National Museum. After hearing some speeches, the crowd decided to march to City Hall and to demand the acceptance of the Twelve Points from the Pest City Council.

The crowd, constantly increasing in size, moved to the City Hall. Again a committee was selected to present the demands. It is significant that in addition to the radicals, who were the sole leaders of the morning demonstration, we now find two prominent liberal nobles from the Opposition on this committee, Gábor Klauzál and Pál Nyári, a leading Pest county official who was highly regarded by the patriots.

The committee found the City Council in session. The Council Hall became "filled with people" and in the square below the crowd sounded like a "roaring sea before the storm."[21] The City Council under these circumstances, was not hostile. The chairman, Pest's Vice-Burgomaster Rottenbiller, greeted the committee as those "bringing the hope of complete freedom" and expressed the expectation that under its protection the city "would remain free of disturbances."[22] Then he signed the Twelve Points and from the window showed the signed copy to the crowd below which shouted its approval.[23]

At Rottenbiller's suggestion, a Committee of Public Safety was formed to maintain order. It included the radicals Petőfi, Vasvári, Irinyi and Irányi, the liberal nobles P. Nyári and Klauzál, and some City Council members. Rottrenbiller became the chairman.[24]

After more speechmaking, the newly-formed Committee of Public Safety decided to present the Twelve Points to the highest national authority in Buda, the *Consilium Locumtenentiale,* the Vice-Regency Council.

The crowd steadily grew in number. While a few hours earlier, only ten thousand were at the National Museum and from ten to fifteen thousand stood before City Hall, all participants agree that at least twenty thousand marched with the Committee to Buda. Degré wrote: "We marched with unbound enthusiasm up to the fortress where we saw artillery men standing next to their cannons holding burning fuses. The multitude in front of them shouting, 'Long live liberty! Long live equality!"[25]

The crowd must also have made an equally great impression on the gentlemen of the Vice-Regency Council. Reports of the confrontation by both the revolutionaries and the chairman of the Buda Council, Count Ferenc Zichy remain. Zichy stated in his official report to the Palatine, that first Rottenbiller and then Nyári and Klauzál spoke to the Council. Three specific requests were presented: 1. The immediate abolition of censorship; 2. The immediate release of the radical writer Táncsics, and 3. An order by the Council directing the military not to interfere.

As Zichy put it, all these points were presented as "requests."[26] This is corroborated by Petőfi who recorded with anger in his "Historic Notes" that Klauzál, although sent by the revolution, spoke so humbly before the Council that he sounded "like a schoolboy before his teacher," and that if twenty thousand people had not been shouting outside the windows, he might have been thrown out as a begging "armer Reisender."[27] In Petőfi's words, the members of the august Council, hearing the shouts of the crowd, were "pale and shaking" and after consulting each other for five minutes, they agreed to everything.[28]

Zichy admitted that "after the appearance of the crowd in the palace voicing its jubilant shouts, the Royal Council could hardly refuse the above-mentioned requests."

The popular demands were satisfied. Táncsics was released and carried triumphantly to Pest by the cheering crowd. Late that night the people celebrated their victory at the National Theatre.

***

The successes of the people on that day were significant. A handful of young radicals mobilized about twenty thousand in a city of 110,000[29] and led them against the established order. What occurred at the printing shop and especially at the Vice-Regency Council was in open defiance of authority, and the will of these young men was imposed upon the representatives of the old order. The radicals accomplished this by acting at the right moment and by taking action when the liberals would have been content with the collection of signatures. Thus, the will of the radicals became the popular will in Budapest for the day and this made them successful.

A most interesting aspect of the day was the absence of violence. Seemingly, the Vice-Regency Council yielded to polite requests. Although violence is usually a part of a revolution, the mere threat of violence from a disorderly crowd sufficed in Hungary in 1848 to force the established authorities to concede to popular demands.

Although the radical leaders even gained a share in power, this does not seem to have been one of their goals. Petőfi had declared the first step of the revolution to be the freedom of the press, the rest he would leave to others. By twentieth century standards this might sound naïve or even hopelessly romantic. Any revolutionary today would consider the first logical step of a revolution to be the seizure of power. Jókai sensed this. In his memoirs written 25 years later, he tried to relate the events to the special conditions in Hungary. "It is easy to make a revolution in another city. One knows what to do. First, one drives away the government, [then] surrounds the parliament. But where could we get a govermnent and a parliament when our chancellor was in Vienna and our parliament was in Pozsony?"[30] Certainly, these were factors. But, the existing authority, the Vice-Regency Council, was not driven away, only forced to modify existing conditions. The radicals seem to have thought that once official authorization was given, popular wishes were legitimized and the problems were solved. Their concept was similar to that of the French revolutionaries of 1789 who wanted to transform France with the approval of Louis XVI and, also the "good Berliners" of Frederick William IV and the Viennese of 1848, both of whom wanted to abolish censorship and to receive a constitution from their monarch.

The story of March 15 became national legend in Hungary; to this day the average Hungarian thinks of the events of this day when he thinks of 1848. The anniversary of the revolution is celebrated as the national holiday[31] in every town and school. Of all the imprtant events of the revolution, it is worth noting that, like the French celebration of Bastille Day, Hungarians celebrate the day of the people's victory.

In Pozsony, the Diet also moved into action. On March 14, Kossuth took the initiative and announced the news of the Vienna revolution to the Diet. He demanded that the Palatine, now in Pozsony, convene the Upper House and it act on his proposals of March 3[32] at once. Kossuth recommended that immediate steps be taken to introduce legislation insuring freedom of the press and to maintain internal peace.

Kossuth's tone was moderate. He wanted to keep the "reins of the movement" with the Diet and to go only so far as was absolutely necessary to retain that leadership. He urged that the only way to secure the "unavoidable triumph of freedom" without violence and bloodshed was to act without delay. If not, they would be "overcome by the circumstances" and the laws to ensure freedom of the press would not be written in the legislature but elsewhere.[33]

Kossuth was convincing. That day the Upper House voted unanimously in favor of his March 3 proposals. Now, both Houses had recognized the necessity of the complete abolition of feudalism and the establishment of a modern, independent parliamentary government for Hungary. The Lower House passed additional reform bills on the 14th and early on the 16th of March. The old regime was superseded by direct popular action in the capital and it came to an end legally in the halls of the Diet in Pozsony.

The Diet then took action to gain the King's acceptance. A delegation comprising members from both Houses took the steamship up the Danube to Vienna. In Vienna, Kossuth and his fellow delegates were given an enthusiastic reception by the public.[34] The Palatine presented the Hungarian case to the Court. Archduke Stephen, a cousin of the King, recommended satisfaction of the Hungarian demands as necessary "if we want to avoid anarchy and a republic." He considered the situation such that "either we make a favorable decision or we lose this province!" He added that he could not return to Pozsony without acceptance of the demands.[35]

Under this pressure, the Court yielded. Ferdinand stated in a letter to the Palatine that, upon learning the wishes of his faithful Hungarian nation and following the clear dictates of his paternal heart, he would "direct his thoughts" to the satisfaction of Hungarian national desires. In the same letter, he also gave plenipotentiary powers to Archduke Stephen and specifically authorized him to appoint "suitable" men to the independent and responsible Hungarian government. This was to be done, of course, while retaining the "unity of the Crown and territorial integrity of the Empire."[36]

It seems safe to assume that the "clear dictates of his paternal heart" were strongly influenced by the fact that Vienna was also in the hands of revolutionaries and —as Archduke Stephen expressed it—anarchy and a republic might be the outcome if the proposals were not met. Fear of anarchy and further revolution made the Court conciliatory and secured the demands of the Hungarian delegation.

On March 17, armed with the King's letter, Archduke Stephen appointed Count Lajos Batthyány, the official head of the Opposition, as Prime Minister of the first independent responsible government of Hungary. Batthyány was authorized to "recommend members of his cabinet for the highest confirmation."[37]

The permission to form a Hungarian cabinet represented a great victory for the Diet and, since the Diet was under Kossuth's leadership, for Kossuth personally. All Hungary recognized this. Even Kossuth's opponent, Széchenyi, admitted that Kossuth had gained more for the country by his quick action than his own policies could have produced in 20 years.[38] When the delegation had returned to Pozsony, the Diet enacted bills to abolish feudalism and to establish a parliamentary state.

# CHAPTER IV
# REVOLUTIONARY CHANGES IN BUDAPEST AFTER MARCH 15 AND THE INVOLVEMENT OF THE PEASANTS

While the Diet drew up and passed legislation in Pozsony, revolutionary spirit mounted in Budapest. Popular meetings and demonstrations took place daily and the public, having discovered its power on March 15, was reluctant to return to its former passivity. On March 16 the artisans stopped work. The printers, among them Landerer, staged a demonstration. Dressed in the traditional blue blouses of the working man, they marched in the streets carrying the Hungarian colors and a big sign inscribed: "Long live freedom of the press!" They were cheered wildly by the bystanders.[1]

The following day the university students met and proposed that the University of Budapest be independent from the University of Vienna and thoroughly reorganized. They demanded academic freedom, appointments to the faculty to be made solely on the basis of merit, not patronage, and the retirement of old outdated professors. Even the rector of the University signed the students' petition which they planned to present to the Diet along with the Twelve Points.[2]

In this atmosphere, even confirmed conservatives changed their attitudes, or at least pretended to do so. A contemporary pamphleteer, who described the early events of the revolution, wrote that even Louis Philippe had not been deserted by the French conservatives as rapidly as the public officials in Budapest left their conservative ways. "Our great lords, the aristocrats with coats of arms, suddenly became democrats with national cockades."[3] Even ecclesiastics and the Conservative Club attempted to join the Opposition Circle. Little wonder that Petőfi happily wrote to a fellow poet: "There is revolution, my friend, and you can imagine how much I am in my element!"[4]

The young radicals became popular heroes overnight and exercised the greatest influence in the capital. Degré mentions in his memoirs that Petőfi, Jókai, Vasvári, Bulyovszky, Irinyi, Irányi, Rottenbiller and himself spoke at the daily popular meetings held in front of the Museum.[5] The extent of the radicals control over public opinion becomes clear from the testimony of their conservative opponents who hated all that the radicals stood for. An informed Court official in Vienna, Baron Jósika, complained in a letter of March 24 that the "dictatorship" of Petőfi, Irinyi, Irányi and Vasvári overshadowed even the prestige of the Prime Minister in Budapest and that these men exercised the "greatest terrorism."[6]

Zichy, head of the Vice-Regency Council, in official reports to the Viennese Court wrote that "open republican tendencies" had appeared in Pest and that not an hour passed without some new excitement under the leadership of the radicals.[7] Palatine Archduke Stephen wrote to the King that in Pest "anarchy reigned" and that the royal authorities had lost power since the Committee of Public Safety had been established.[8]

Public meetings, demonstrations, speechmaking and the Committee of Public Safety all might truly appear to a Habsburg prince and aristocratic Court officials as anarchy. They do not mention violence or atrocities, however, as there were none. The Committee really did exercise power in Budapest. The "dictatorship" and "terrorism" of the radicals were nothing more than the power of persuasion over the citizenry.

The outward appearance of Budapest had changed greatly. The national colors were displayed on every house. People wore red, white and green cockades and the radicals added "immense red feathers" in their hats. "Everyone carried a sword on the street: students took them to school and actors took them to rehearsals." Petőfi walked about with such a large one, it was mockingly called a "guillotine" by his friends. Also, the Pilvax received a new name: it became the "Hall of Liberty."[9]

It took only four days from the start of the revolution for the radicals to put out their own newspaper which they named after the great day, *Marczius Tizenötödike (March Fifteenth).* The lead article in the first issue declared that the newspaper had emerged from the glorious day of March 15 and would confine itself for the moment to the exercise of influence in the capital. Its purpose would be "to inform the public as quickly as possible of the daily changes in the political climate and to fight against those outworn ideas which preceded March 15."[10]

A coincidental factor which added to the extraordinary nature of those days was the presence of several thousand peasants at a state-wide market held annually in the middle of March in the field of Rákos on the outskirts of Budapest. Perhaps this event prompted Petőfi to write another poem which was then in circulation entitled "Glorious Great Lords."[11] In it, Petőfi threatens the nobility with a peasant war. The nobles are told that they have treated the serfs like animals for centuries and are asked what if the serfs retaliated like wild beasts taking vengeance for the thousand years of suffering. Petőfi envisaged a war to settle the accounts between the nobility and peasantry. He also addressed the peasants and urged that their behavior be superior to that of their former masters if the nobility accepted them as brothers and recognized them as equals. He urged the peasants to extend their hands in friendship as the fatherland had need of all.

The last stanza makes clear Petőfi's threat:

"We have no time to wait
You [must act] quickly
The time is at hand
Tomorrow may be too late.
If you still
Hold us in comtempt
The Lord God should have mercy on you."

This poem apparently gave credence to a rumor which spread in the Diet and all over Hungary that a peasant army was encamped near the capital. The rumor claimed that thirty to forty thousand peasants were ready to attack the nobility under Petőfi's leadership.[12]

It seems that the nobility in Hungary experienced a sort of "Great Fear" in March of 1848. Unfounded rumors were enough to encourage many nobles to move to the cities.[13] Prime Minister Batthyány's first communication reflected their concern. He ordered municipal and county authorities to "maintain peace and order by the energetic use of their authority and influence and utilization of every means except those of violence." He ordered the strict application of laws to insure the work of the Cabinet and Diet would not be disturbed by "excesses and premature demands."[14]

By "excesses and premature demands" Batthyány meant that action by the peasants to abolish serfdom should be avoided at all cost. His whole political career had been spent fighting feudalism but he wanted reforms to be carried out legally, constitutionally and peacefully. And Batthyány was not alone.

Baron Wesselényi, a reform leader and outstanding patriot who had been imprisoned by the Metternich government, wrote to Kossuth on March 23 that a "somewhat educated and intelligent" populace was needed for the great transformation but that such a group did not exist in Hungary.

"The village populace hardly felt the intellectual oppression which the reforms worked to correct with such success. The oppression of poverty cannot be cured so quickly. The unfortunate one learns easily from the "National Song" that we 'swear that we shall not be

> slaves anymore!' But, it can be interpreted also that, upon swearing this oath, he no longer had to obey either his county superiors or estate-owner."[15]

Fear of the peasants had a salutary effect on the Diet in Pozsony. It proceeded with great dispatch and on March 18 both Houses passed a bill which abolished forever feudal obligations.[16] A member of the Lower House wrote that the quick action was due to a "certain kind of *panique (sic)* created by both the circulating rumors and Petőfi's "really mad poem."[17] In a private note the Palatine wrote the bill 'went through both Houses in the first fright" and that if the King did not veto it, it would be the ruin of the nobility.[18]

In Vienna, Baron Jósika stated that the "decisions of the Diet were enacted out of fear of a peasant uprising which was widely rumored but never materialized."[19] He even charged that "preparations had been made to mislead the public," presumably believing that there was a conspiracy.

Apart from Petőfi's "mad" poem, there is no evidence that the radicals tried to incite the peasants. Perhaps the nobles connected the presence of the peasants at Rákos with the revolution in Budapest. But, the poem, the presence of the peasants and, it seems, their own uneasy consciences, caused the nobles to act so quickly.[20]

Petőfi indicated in his diary his awareness of his national reputation and readiness to lead the peasants:

> "The Diet abolished feudal obligations. It was about time! They had received the news that Sándor Petőfi was camping at Rákos along with 40,000 peasants and this pleasant surprise induced them to the largesse of abolishing feudalism. The news of Rákos was without foundation. But, if the honorable gentlemen had not acted as they did, I can assure them in my name that the baseless news would have soon had foundation with the exception that perhaps not 40,000 but twice that number, or even more, would have gathered at Rákos."[21]

# CHAPTER V
# TOWARD DUAL POWER EXERCISED BY THE DIET AND THE COMMITTEE OF PUBLIC SAFETY IN BUDAPEST

The revolutionary activity in Budapest was to a great extent spontaneous. The radicals primarily influenced public opinion by speaking at popular meetings and participating in demonstrations. But they also took part in exercising administrative authority as members of the newly-created Committee of Public Safety.

The Committee held a meeting late the evening of March 15[1] and the decisions show that the Committee was very much under the sway of its radical members. Two proclamations were issued. One informed the people of Budapest of the establishment of the Committee and the accomplishments of the revolution. It called for the illumination of the city the next day to celebrate the "magnificent victory of reform."[2]

The other proclamation established a National Guard, open to "every honest man" and promised free weapons and identification. The Committee urged the residents to follow the instructions of the National Guard.[3] The proclamation concluded with "Long live the King! Constitutional reform, liberty, equality, peace and order!"[4] But, there was little question that the Committee had established the National Guard not to cheer the King but rather to keep his soldiers from the city. In arming the people, the Committee was preparing for all eventualitites.

The call for a National Guard was answered warmly and the Committee's efforts were directed to its organization. The morning of March 16 the enlistment of volunteers at recruiting stations began.[5] The greatest problem was the shortage of arms, available only from the military authorities with the approval of the Vice-Regency Council. As in Paris in 1789 and in Vienna on March 13, it was one of those anomalous situations when the people had to get their weapons from the very ones against whom they might be used. With the Council's permission, 500 muskets were obtained on March 16 and the next day the commandment of the Buda garrison, Baron Lederer gave over another 1,000.[6] He also gave his word of honor that no more remained in the arsenal.[7]

There were many more volunteers than arms. Those who could afford it equipped themselves. They drilled in the public squares and "kept order at popular meetings and patrolled the city day and night."[8] On March 18, all guard members took an oath to be faithful to the fatherland, King and constitution.[9] It is worth noting that the fatherland took precedence over the King.

The Committee of Public Safety secured the support of the municipal council of Buda which broadened its popular base and gave the Committee "legal" jurisdiction over the capital.[10] Its early decisions indicate a certain ambivalence. On the one hand measures were directed toward organizing the revolution and keeping revolutionary zeal alive. On the other hand great emphasis was placed on the maintenance of order.

The national rights of Hungary were asserted by the Committee. Imperial colors and coats-of-arms were removed from public buildings and were replaced by the national tricolor to general popular acclaim. The official language of the royal treasury was changed from Latin to Hungarian. Passage of two seemingly innocuous measures represented a real victory to the masses: certain tobacco shops were closed and the state lottery suspended.[11] The government-sponsored tobacco shops were one of the most unpopular features of the Viennese bureaucracy throughout the Habsburg Monarchy. In Milan, the first protests against absolutism took the form of a campaign among the patriots to stop smoking and to cease participating in the state lottery.[12] There, the controversy over tobacco led to bloody clashes with Radetzky's soldiers; in Budapest, the Vice-Regency Council capitulated, tobacco shops were closed and the lottery ended without incident.

For the purpose of propaganda, the Committee had 10,000 copies of the "National Song" printed[13] and at Petőfi's suggestion the square before City Hall was renamed Liberty Square as was the street where Landerer's printing shop was located and the square before the university was called March 15 Square.[14]

The Committee rejected a petition submitted on March 18 requesting that the enlistment of Jews in the National Guard be discontinued. Upholding the principle of equality, the Committee merely recomcended that Jewish volunteers enlist in the section organized at the Opposition Circle where they would be welcomed.[15]

Petőfi wrote in his diary on March 20:

> "The concord which had reigned has started to disintegrate. German citizens, I accuse you before the nation and posterity of causing

> it to disintegrate. As the first to declare they would not accept a Jew among themselves in the National Guard, they were the first to throw mud at the virgin flag of March 15."[16]

Petőfi cried indignantly that the anti-Semites were a few disreputable lawyers representing a cause so unjust and shameful that it asked heaven for punishment.

As early as March 17, the Committee issued resolutions to keep a moderate course and to prevent lawlessness. It was resolved that jobless vagrants should be kept under strict police surveillance; taverns should be closed early. Heads of families were urged to supervise their households; jobs were to be provided for as many as possible and the town's butchers were warned against increasing their prices.[17]

No doubt, these measures were intended to avoid independent action on the part of the poor. The size of the Committee had been increased to include a number of rather cautious burghers. More radicals were also added, however, among them Jókai, Bulyovszky and Degré, but the moderate city burghers and liberal nobles were in the majority.[18]

This change in the composition of the Committee is a possible explanation why the Committee reversed itself on the important question of unrestricted enlistment of "honest" men into the National Guard. On March 18, it was resolved that, as it was put, journeymen who were not permanent inhabitants of the city could join only if vouched for by a Guardsman of good repute. As a further restriction, journeymen in the Guard had to be native-born Hungarians[19] in this way eliminating many of the skilled laborers and artisans in Budapest who were Germans by birth.

The Committee reacted cautiously also to a request from a delegation of university students to send agitators to the countryside to "enlighten the people about the revolutionary movement." Nyári denied the request in the name of the Committee. The students demand that all judicial proceedings be opened to the public was also denied by Nyári. He said that such changes could be made only "by law," i.e., the Diet would have to enact such a measure.[20]

The Committee was, however, the personification of the revolution to the country in general and to the Diet in particular when its delegation finally presented the Twelve Points in Pozsony on March 19. Petőfi, Vasvári and Bulyovszky were members but the speaker for the delegation was Pál Hajnik.[21] Hajnik spoke respectfully but made it clear that the people of Budapest were "joined fraternally in all interests, and looked upon the Twelve Points as the pledge for the future prosperity of the country."[22] Along with the Twelve Points, he presented the students' demands for the reorganization of the University of Budapest and he urged the removal of the Diet to Budapest at once.

Széchenyi, who was presiding, asked the deputies for a reply. Kossuth rose immediately and expressed satisfaction with the patriotic fervor in Budapest. (As the idea of the petition had been approved by him, he could hardly say otherwise!) But he added:

> "I consider the population of Budapest extremely important and Budapest the heart of the fatherland. But I will never accept it as the master of the fatherland. This nation possesses liberty and all its members want to be free. Just as the word "nation" cannot be arrogated by one caste, it cannot be arrogated by one city either Fifteen million Hungarians together make the fatherland and the nation."[23]

Kossuth said he hoped that the citizens of Budapest were in agreement and added that the nation was strong enough "to crush" those who might think differently. He pointed out that the Diet presently was acting upon most of the Twelve Points and that future assembly meetings would be held in Budapest but due to the heavy workload and the pressure of time it was inadvisable to make the move now. He closed with the recommendation that the petition should be sent to committee for consideration.

Although Kossuth used friendly terms the thrust of his speech was to uphold the authority and power of the Diet.[24] To remind the delegation that they did not represent the whole nation and that anyone who assumed this position would be crushed were strong words from the leader of the future national revolution.

Possibly Kossuth's remarks were partly intended to reassure his fellow deputies whom he did not want to antagonize. But, it seems, Kossuth's primary interest was in retaining the initiative for reform in the Diet where he was the unquestioned leader. It is reasonable that he would maintain the authority of a legally-constituted body representing the lesser nobility through which he wished to accomplish the modernization of the country. In those days of his triumph, it was unlikely that he would yield to the Budapest radicals.

Although Kossuth had suggested the petition, he did not forsee the consequences: the creation of the Committee of Public Safety, a new power center. In all likelihood he had planned to use the petition for his own purposes against the conservatives who formed almost half of the Lower House and an overwhelming majority in the Upper House. Kossuth probably meant, quite literally, his threat to crush the

Committee if it dared to arrogate nationwide power.

In any event, the radicals in Budapest interpreted his remarks to mean that. In return they questioned the basis for the authority of the Diet. The *March Fifteenth* stated that the deputies in the Diet should not be called "the representatives of the nation," because they had been elected only by one 'caste,' and in some places and in many instances by only a few individuals from that caste."[25] In the same issue but without mention of Kossuth's name, the paper stated:

> "At the diet, among some, words are spoken insinuating that the capital attempts to speak in the name of 15 million. This it did not do. It spoke in its own name but was convinced that the whole country would follow its example. . . . Paris is not France either, but the party which can create general movements in Paris can surely count on the sympathy of the countryside. What the city of Pest did, it did on its own responsibility. We are beginning to live in such times that the people of the capital begin to appear as the country's authorized supervisor over the legislature."[26]

This is the first manifestation of antagonism between the Diet and the revolutionary capital. The Diet had the legal right to speak for the country but the radical newspaper pointed out correctly that it had its mandate only from the nobility, not the population at large. Between the Diet and the Committee of Public Safety, the latter was more representative of the "popular will" because the Committee owed its existence to direct popular action and the continued approval of the people of Budapest. Thus, as long as the legislature was constituted as a feudal body, its moral authority remained open to question.

The deputies, themselves, felt this also. While the delegation from Budapest was at the Diet, a delegation from the Diet[27] including members from both Houses, went to Budapest where they were formally received by the Committee of Public Safety at City Hall. The Pozsony delegation thanked the leaders and the inhabitants of Pest in the name of the estates for their patriotism and courage, stressing especially their worthiness for safeguarding life and property. The delegation spokesman said that, "since they were only the representatives of the nobility," once they had completed the most urgent tasks they would turn over their functions to a new, popularly-elected parliament representative of the whole nation. Until that time, however, all were exhorted to obey and trust the government of Count Batthyány.[28]

The liberal noble, Pál Nyári, gave a most interesting reply. He reminded the delegation from the Diet that they were living in eventful times but that they had not witnessed the greatest event: March 15 in Budapest! He urged them to legislate "without delay" the demands contained in the Twelve Points.[29]

The fact that the Diet sent a delegation to Budapest implied recognition of the revolution. The legal authority in Hungary, the Diet, treated with the revolution's Committee almost as with an equal. Instead of being grateful for the gesture, one Committee member told the Pozsony delegation to get on with their work and satisfy the popular demands. The Committee was beginning to behave as an "authorized supervisor" over the Diet.

On March 19 a bill dealing with freedom of the press was submitted and accepted at the Diet. It abolished censorship but required newspapers to deposit the sum of 20,000 forints as security against slander and other press offenses. It made the writers, the publisher and even the printing shop responsible and liable for what was printed.[30] The bill typified the thinking of early nineteenth century liberals who believed in granting rights on the basis of wealth.

When the contents of the bill became known in Budapest, it caused the "greatest consternation" among the people and led to an angry demonstration. The *March Fifteenth* graphically described the scene:

> "At 4:00 p.m. in front of City Hall some units of the National Guard stood at arms. The youth and the people were in an indescribable state of irritation. . . . A new unit of the Guard, the armed youth of the University arrived. Some Guard members sent for torches. The press bill was read aloud. Each article was greeted with loud shouts of disapproval and then the Diet's bill was publicly burned."[31]

The Committee of Public Safety, meeting inside City Hall, immediately sent a special courier to Pozsony to demand the revision of the bill. The Committee also declared itself to be a "permanent" body until the establishment of a popularly-elected parliament in Budapest.[32]

The news of the demonstration and the Committee's action forced the Diet to reconsider the bill. The law was modified and the required security deposit was cut in half. It was now apparent that the Committee, supported by the citizens of Budapest, could exert decisive pressure on the Diet.[33]

The Committee received support from the country in general. Revolutionary committees were spontaneously formed in dozens of cities and, in many instances, took over the local administration on the model of Pest and organized National Guard units. Even in Pozsony, a Committee of Public Safety was formed, which served as a reminder to the nobles that the revolution was by no means confined to Budapest.[34]

Committees in the provincial towns were quick to establish contact with the Committee of Public Safety in Budapest.[35] Some sent written greetings with assurances of cooperation. Others sent delegations to make personal contact. One district offered to put its forces under the command of the Budapest Committee if the need arose.[36] The Budapest Committee steadily gained in prestige and became known as the "Central Committee."

The Central Committee received strong support from a new Committee representing Pest county.[37] Pál Nyári was president of the new Committee and among the members were Petőfi, Jókai, Irinyi and Degré. The great majority of the members came from the liberal opposition. At its first meeting the Committee abolished all titles except those of the ruling house. But most important, every inhabitant of the county was given the "right of counsel and vote" in the Council room of Pest county.[38] This introduced universal suffrage in the largest and most important administrative unit of Hungary, an unprecedented phenomenom in the country's history.

Thus, in about one week, a rather curious situation had developed. The Diet in Pozsony was enacting bills ostensibly to meet the demands of the revolutionary capital. If the population of Budapest and its Central Committee disapproved of the legislation—and made their displeasure known—the Diet would reconsider the bill to make it more acceptable. There seemed to be a kind of dual power in Hungary at this time with the Diet having lost the initiative. To those in Budapest, this loss of initiative became even more apparent when a National Guard was established by the Diet on March 22. The Diet was, in fact, only legalizing what had already become a reality in Budapest and numerous other cities.

But, again the Diet attempted to exercise a restrictive and moderating influence. To the nobles, the arming of all people seemed dangerous. Some deputies wished to restrict recruitment; others did not like the idea in any form. Fears were voiced over setting the qualifications too low since "emissaries advocating communistic ideas could join and who would be able to guarantee that they would not turn their arms against the estate owners?"[39]

Kossuth had to point out that the Diet was, more or less, giving belated approval to an existing fact. He told them it would be extremely difficult to disarm those who already had weapons.[40] He could not persuade his fellow deputies to lower the requirements, however, and the bill was passed restricting membership in the Guard to those with either an annual income of 200 forints or considerable property in the countryside.[41] The bill did not result in changes in the composition of the National Guard in Budapest and only prompted a declaration from the revolutionary committee of Pest county that men would continue to be enlisted without property qualifications.[42]

When the Diet tried to exercise influence, it was disregarded by the revolutionaries, whose paper was calling for the dissolution of the Diet. "The Committee of Public Safety can decide the fate of the nation. It represents the brave people of the capital and possesses the fraternal support of the Hungarian-speaking regions of the country. . . . The diet should cease functioning and should not speak in the name of the people it does not represent."[43]

Prime Minister Batthyány was unable to resolve the rivalry between Pest and Pozsony. He was in Pozsony forming the first Cabinet and had included the most prominent members of the former liberal opposition: Kossuth, Széchenyi, Deák, Klauzál, Eötvös and Szemere. To this group was added Colonel Mészáros, a cavalry officer, and Prince Esterházy, a former ambassador to the Court of St. James and the wealthiest man in Hungary. The most determined member of the Cabinet was Kossuth, the Minister of Finance, and the only man fully acceptable to Budapest radicals.

Although the Cabinet had not yet been confirmed by the Crown and in a strict sense could not be considered legal, it did attempt to take over the administration in Budapest. At Batthyány's suggestion, the Palatine authorized two of the designated cabinet ministers, Szemere and Klauzál, to form a provisional ministerial group for the maintenence of order in Budapest.[44] During the following days, Szemere and Klauzál stayed in Budapest but the Committee of Public Safety had no intention of relinquishing its power and continued to maintain its key role with every means at its command. The revolution's Committee was not ready to abdicate.[45]

## CHAPTER VI
## UNEASY ALLIANCE BETWEEN DIET AND COMMITTEE AND THEIR MUTUAL VICTORY OVER THE VIENNA COURT

In the ten days since March 15 considerable tension had developed between the Diet and the Committee of Public Safety. The early manifestations of a counterrevolution, however, altered the political picture. The first counterrevolutionary plan came from the Palatine Archduke Stephen, the King-Emperor's representative holding plenipotentiary powers. As early as March 24, in a memorandum to Ferdinand, the Archduke analyzed the current developments and presented possible plans of action.[1] Stating that the political situation was so grave that "...one could expect the most dangerous outbreak at any time. . . .and that anarchy reigned in Pest and local authorities had lost their power after the establishment of the Committee of Public Safety," Archduke Stephen contemplated three possible moves. The first was to remove all troops from the country and leave it to its fate, probably resulting in a peasant uprising against the nobility. The second was to reach an agreement with Batthyány. The third was the use of military force requiring at least 40-50,000 men. The troops could be sent to Pozsony under the command of a royal commissioner empowered with *ius gladii* to dissolve the Diet. The troops would take Pest and keep the nation under the "iron fist of the military."

The Archduke considered the first possibility unacceptable because it would harm the nobility and the third alternative difficult to implement because of the lack of money, troops and the possiblity of disturbances arising in other parts of the Empire. He strongly urged the second solution: to come to an agreement with Batthyány. He stated that the dynasty need not honor the agreement forever and, "later, if better times follow" the concessions granted could be revoked.[2]

As only a few days earlier Archduke Stephen had advised the monarch to veto the Diet's bill liberating the serfs, a plan to turn back the revolutionary tide begins to emerge. While secretly making these recommendations to his King, the Archduke gave every ostensible appearance of being a Hungarian patriot and he even received credit from the public for securing royal approval for Count Batthyány's appointment as Prime Minister.

A new source of conflict between Pozsony and Budapest developed over the Diet's limited suffrage bill. The new bill granted voting rights, for the first time in Hungarian history, to commoners who could meet certain property and education requirements and meanwhile assured the voting rights of those who already had them.[3] The radicals took exception to the bill because as it was formulated only commoners would have to meet property and education requirements while the nobles retained their rights even if they did not fulfill these requirements.

The Committee of Public Safety discussed the bill in a lengthy session.[4] All the radicals agreed that it was not inclusive enough. Nyári denounced the bill as "contrary to the principle of equality" and predicted that it would lead to internal disturbances. The radical noble, Mór Perczel, claimed that "bloody conflict" would follow from this "mummification" of the rights of the nobility. Vasvári, usually very radical, declared that the "sun of liberty should shine on everyone" but, in order to prevent a "proletarian[5] flood" he favored modest property qualifications. Jókai stressed the great importance of the "proletarians" and considered age and permanent residence sufficient requirements. Only one of the radicals, the Francophile Irányi, demanded "suffrage universelle" (*sic*).

Although the Diet's bill was opposed by all Committee members there was no agreement on an alternative. The degree of democracy they wished to establish was not clear in their own minds. They did lean toward a law requiring low property qualifications applied equally to noble and commoner. This, the Diet would not grant. No concensus was reached by the Committee but it sent a courier, the radical Degré, to Pozsony to urge passage of a suffrage law with the "widest possible basis."

Opposition to the proposed property qualification was voiced in *March Fifteenth* which printed the following criticism of the electoral law: "Under these laws, it may easily happen that those who belong in the national assembly the most, the men of the people with something new to say, will be excluded. Democratic thinking will be excluded. The real friends of the people will be ignored."[6] The protest was ignored as the public's attention was drawn to the first counterrevolutionary move made by the Court.

Two royal communiqués to the Diet were issued on March 28.[7] The first expressed the Court's reservations to the establishment of a separate cabinet for Hungary. Ferdinand rejected the idea of separate Hungarian Ministries of Finance and War. He wished all revenues from Hungary be sent to the Vienna central treasury and said that the control of the army was a royal prerogative for the maintenance of the Pragmatic Sanction and the territorial integrity of Hungary.

In the second communiqué the King accepted the liberation of the serfs "in principle" but did not wish them to stop working for the nobles immediately which would cause considerable hardship to the nobility and disrupt production. He asked the Diet to reconsider the proposed bill, taking his observations under advisement, and to include specific provisions for compensation to the nobility. The same procedure should be followed with regard to the bill abolishing the tithe.

Since Ferdinand had promised 12 days earlier to accept an independent Hungarian Cabinet and certain reforms, the royal communiques meant the revocation of at least part of what had been granted. This stand of the Court had strong repercussions in Hungary. Even before the royal declarations were issued, rumors had been circulating in Budapest that the King was planning to deny separate war and finance ministries. On March 27, at Nyári's suggestion, the Committee of Public Safety issued the following declaration addressed to the nation:

> "The friends of the old oppressive system wish to induce the King To take the military and financial matters—the nerve and blood of the; nation—out of the hands of the Hungarian national government and thus, break his royal word.
>
> "We emphatically protest against this denial to the nation of its rightful demands.
>
> "The Pragmatic Sanction, mutually guarantees the rights of the nation and the ruling house but this is a two-way bond. Until now, only one part of it has been maintained: that one dealing with the interests of the ruling house. At present, it is necessary to secure the independence of our government so the other part can be observed also and that is to secure the rights of the nation.
>
> "The nation has given its blood to save one part of the Pragmatic Sanction and it will do the same, if necessary, to save the other part too."[8]

The proclamation placed the blame on the King's advisors for the reversal of his promises but it was the dynasty that was threatened with war if the national demands were not satisfied.

At the same session the proclamation was issued, definite proposals for the national role the Committee was to play were formulated. A radical actor, Gábor Egressy, moved that representation on the Committee be extended to all cities which had sent expressions of solidarity. The motion failed when it was pointed out that at the moment delegates from other cities were included the "national convent" (*sic*) would be proclaimed and it was not yet time. The Committee could afford to wait a few days. Another motion to contact the provinces by sending out couriers also failed because the Committee did not have the funds.[9] The *March Fifteenth* dryly commented, "We know how to be enthusiastic, but we have not learned how to make [financial] sacrifices yet."[10]

Excitement in the city continued to mount in the next two days. One public meeting followed another and Zichy reported to Vienna that not one hour passed without new commotion. He added: "I can assure Your Excellency that if favorable decisions, particularly in regard to the Ministries of Finance and War, are not made, Hungary is lost. Yesterday afternoon, because the Cabinet has not yet been appointed, open republican tendencies were manifested."[11]

Zichy named Petőfi, Jókai, Vasvári and Nyári as the leaders of the popular demonstrations and he even suggested the possibility that Archduke Stephen might be declared king in Budapest if the Court did not satisfy the national demands.

Meanwhile, Petőfi, Jókai and Vasvári kept the public informed at mass meetings held on the square in front of the National Museum. These meetings, attended by tens of thousands of people, prepared the population of the capital psychologicially for open defiance.

At the end of March, Petőfi published another outstanding political poem in which he attacked the institution of the monarchy as well as the person of the monarch. In "To the Kings" he compared the monarchy to a tree whose fruit was overripe and rotten. He warned the kings that the people would tolerate them as a necessary evil only for a short while, and that the day of judgment was approaching. The basic idea of the poem was stated in the refrain:

> "No matter what impudent flatterers say,
> There is no *beloved* King anymore."[12]

This poem was widely circulated and quoted and added to the general unrest in the capital. It also had consequences for Petőfi's political future.

While Petőfi and others were arousing the people, the Committee followed up its proclamation to the nation and sent two of its members with a message to the Diet. In the message, the Committee served notice that if Hungary did not receive a favorable answer on the Cabinet appointments within 24 hours, the Pragmatic Sanction would be declared null and void in Budapest. The Committee invited those deputies who wanted to participate in decision-making on the country's future to come to the capital as ti had been decided to hold a national convent there.[13]

This decision, another example of the Diet's loss of initiative, is even more noteworthy because it was a step toward national unity to protect the revolution from foreign interference. But there is no indication that it occurred to the radicals to offer their support to the Diet in the name of national unity. Instead, it was the radicals who told the deputies to come to Budapest. The radicals wanted national unity but under their own leadership. In all probability, if the Diet in Pozsony had submitted to the Crown, the nation would have accepted the radical's leadership.

The determined stand by the Budapest Committee left the Diet little alternative if the deputies wished to have any political influence in the country. When the royal communiqués finally arrived in Pozsony on March 29, even the moderate Batthyány denounced them and threatened to resign if they remained unchanged.[14] Archduke Stephen solemnly gave his word that they would be changed or he would give up his office.[15] An interesting remark from one who, only five days earlier, had submitted a secret plan for counterrevolution. Kossuth, as usual, delivered the speech with the greatest impact. He declared that no delay in the liberation of the serfs would be tolerated. He believed the royal answer concerning the Cabinet endangered the future of the throne and the nation. Kossuth gave a strong warning that the people might lose their faith in the royal word and—alluding to the situation in Budapest—said that the "blood of the citizens might flow."[16] After more speechmaking, the Diet produced two strongly-worded resolutions echoing Kossuth's words.[17] The resolutions were taken to Vienna by the Palatine, Batthyány, Deák and Eötvös, all moderate patriots. A good deal would depend upon the answer they would bring back from the Court.

While the delegation from the Diet was in Vienna, Budapest received the full text of the royal communiqués. The news precipitated an outburst of popular indignation and a demonstration of unprecedented anger and magnitude took place. "Groups started to form verywhere in the streets and one could hear, 'We were cheated in Vienna.' 'We don't want a German government.' 'Long live the national convent.' 'To arms! To arms!' And it was said for the first time 'Long live the republic!'"[18]

One group attempted to break into a church in the center of town in order to sound the tocsin.[19] The largest group, however, marched to City Hall and demanded arms from the Committee at once.[20] At City Hall another excited group carrying a red flag, also wanted to sound the tocsin from the tower and to hoist the red flag over the building.[21] Only armed National Guardsmen, among the Jókai, were able to restrain them.

Apparently, the crowd wanted, above all, arms. There was little need for such urgency, however, as there was no immediate threat from the "enemy" in Vienna. But ordinary logic ceases to function with excited masses and it became clear that some action was needed to pacify the crowds.

According to Pulszky, Kossuth's designated Undersecretary of Finance, he, Nyári and Rottenbiller put into effect a plan to talk to the crowd until the people grew weary. They gave speeches denouncing Vienna and protesting the infringement of Hungary's rights.[22] But they also suggested to the crowd that they should defer action until the results of the Diet's delegation in Vienna became known.[23] Although the speakers were frequently interrupted by the audience, they did succeed in pacifying the demonstrators. In Pulszky's estimation, only the moderating influence of popular politicians prevented the "declaration of a provisional government as had happened in Paris."[24]

However, the demonstration did result in the Committee issuing an important proclamation to the people advising them to be prepared to defend the fatherland.[25] And, for the first time, the Committee asked for allegiance from outside Budapest: "You cities in the countryside, being aware that the fate of the whole country is being decided in Pest, unite with Budapest through your delegates!" Just a few days earlier, the Committee had rejected the idea of direct contact with the provincial cities in the belief it would have amounted to the creation of a national convent. Now, the Committee was making such a bid for power.

Although the Committee was claiming Budapest to be the center of political activity, it did not want to eliminate the Diet from participating in the decision-making. The proclamation concluded with: "Patriots! Our foremost task is to wait, fully prepared, until our fellow countrymen struggling in Pozsony return with good or bad news, then together with them it will be possible to decide the nation's fate."[26]

The phrase "together with them" meant again national unity against counterrevolution, under the leadership of the radicals. There was a real possibility of this. Degré had seen Kossuth recently in Pozsony and came away with the message that if the national cause was shipwrecked in Vienna, Kossuth would come to Budapest to lead the "youth" himself.[27] In such a contingency, Kossuth would have been probably followed by most of the deputies. He most likely would have dominated the scene in the capital, but would have had to share leadership with the Committee. If the Court had not backed down at the end of March, Hungary would probably have witnessed a much more rapid radicalization.

The popular demonstrations, the threats against the dynasty, the openly republican tendencies and the determined stand of the Diet induced the Court to yield. The Camarilla realized that, with its troubles in Vienna and the revolution in Italy, it could ill afford to provoke Hungary also. On March 31, in a new communication to the Palatine,[28] Ferdinand recognized the rights of the Hungarian Ministry of War. Furthermore, he asked the estates to make temporary provision for sending revenues for the maintenence of the Court, diplomatic service and army. He promised that the final arrangements for Hungary's contribution to the common expenses of the Empire would be reached by mutual negotiations between the Court and the next legislature.

This was a clever move on the part of the Habsburgs. They lost some prestige by giving in, but they averted the danger of losing the country. Since the Hungarian demands were granted, there was no longer any cause for war, at least for the moment.

Kossuth and the Diet were completely satisfied with the Court's reply. After reading the document, Kossuth declared to the Diet that "everything was granted which could be granted on paper" and the "rest will be up to the strength of the nation." He agreed with the King's request for monies and suggested that a considerable sum be forwarded to the King for his personal expenses. He also proposed that Ferdinand come to Pozsony to close the last meeting of the estates and witness the determination of the Hungarian nation in the cause of freedom as well as in its loyalty and faithfulness to its King.[29]

The Diet shared Kossuth's feelings and, it seemed, so did a majority in the country. Even in Budapest, unrest decreased considerably. Although the *March Fifteenth* wrote that the royal communiqué of March 31 satisfied no one, it quickly added that it strengthened the government and provided for a viable parliament.[30] According to Petőfi, "The youth, and thus the whole revolution, was very dissatisfied, but the peaceful citizens were pleased and declared almost openly that those who seemed restless were traitors." The following remarks in his diary indicate that Petőfi understood the nature of revolutions better than many:

"Very well, we do not want to be traitors. We will step down and go home. But, if you are not able to suceed with this royal communiqué, then it is you who will be the traitors. You, who dampened the enthusiasm of the youth which is the country's only hope. . . . My young friends. . . goodbye. . . the revolution has ended. . . but no, the revolution is not over, this was but the first act. . . . See you later."[31]

His prediction that the revolution would continue sounded improbable; a peaceful program of reform was the general expection.

The Committee of Public Safety continued to direct the affairs of the capital but attention turned to the Diet in Pozsony where new reforms were being legislated. The King approved Batthyány's Cabinet and the bill liberating the serfs on April 7. There was no further talk of establishing a national convent or a provisional government and it was expected that the government would soon transfer to Budapest and assume control there.

Ferdinand came to Pozsony on April 11 and closed the last meeting of the estates among demonstrations of loyalty to the Crown.[32] Three days later the Batthyány Government transferred its offices to the capital. The ministers, arriving by boat, were greeted at the Danube by a very large crowd. Vasvári welcomed them in the name of 160,000 free citizens of Budapest and proudly pointed to the accomplishments of the March revolution which had destroyed absolutism in the city. He said:

"We have prepared the way. . . .Our revolutionary movement lasted exactly one month. . . .The people will return tomorrow to private life. They now place the power of the revolution in your hands and entrust the fate of the nation to your responsibility. You will have to account for your actions to a powerful reborn nation. Therefore, we call your attention to the holy cause of the fatherland."[33]

Indeed, the scene was symbolic. A radical revolutionary and organizer of the March 15 events welcomed the Government and placed the power of the revolution in its hands. It appeared the revolution was over. The Committee of Public Safety held its last meeting on April 15. It was dissolved by the Government, which assumed administration over the capital and Hungary. The victory of Pozsony over Budapest seemed complete.

***

This victory, however, was only part of a great victory which the Diet, under the leadership of Kossuth, and the revolutionary capital, under the leadership of the radicals, had jointly achieved over the Habsburg Court. The tangible results of the victory were the so-called "April Laws" which embodied the legislative work of the Diet between March 16 and April 11. These laws, duly passed by both Houses, approved and signed by the King, and supported by the vast majority of Hungarians, constituted a drastic departure from the nation's past.

Ancient privileges of the nobility were abolished and equality before the law was established. Serfdom, with its monetary payments, forced labor and personal dependence, was replaced by free ownership of the land, equality of taxation, the disappearance of the tithe, and new civil rights for many people was the new order.

The King, henceforth, would exercise executive power through a Cabinet which was responsible to a popularly-elected parliament. Nearly one half of the adult male population of the country had been enfranchised. The Cabinet, including Ministers of Finance and War, was independent of Vienna. The relationship between Austria and Hungary was reduced to a person union.[34]

This transformation took place with the monarch's most reluctant approval and was due, above all, to the general atmosphere of unrest in Europe at that time. The spring of 1848 turned the old order upside down in Europe. The victorious revolution in France established a republic. The revolution in Berlin forced Frederick William to talk about merging Prussia into Germany, and the burning of a few castles in the countryside made the princes of the smaller German states realize the necessity for reform.

Habsburg power in Italy was challenged by successful revolutions in Milan and Venice, and the armies of Radetzky had to face the Sardinian troops as well as the rebellious inhabitants of Lombardy and Venetia. Even the loyal Viennese had risen up and forced the resignation of Metternich, Europe's living symbol of conservatism.

The collapse of the established order on the continent had its repercussions in Hungary. The Diet in Pozsony exploited the European situation to Hungary's advantage. The generally-deplored semi-dependent status of Hungary had been part of the Metternich system and it was reasonable to expect the Hungarian politicians show their dissatisfication with the status quo after Metternich's fall from power.

The Habsburgs' armies were deployed abroad and, if this had not been the case, it is unlikely that Hungarian demands would have been acceded to without a serious struggle.

In terms of power, in Europe in March 1848, revolutionary zeal proved itself stronger than the police and military establishments of the rulers. But foreign revolutions alone would not have provided sufficient strength for Kossuth and the Diet to act if Budapest had not been taken over by the revolutionaries under radical leadership.

Kossuth and the Diet strictly adhered to the legal forms and wished to accomplish reform through legislative action within the framework of the constitution. In some respects, this was their great strength. They never felt the embarassment suffered by the liberals in the Frankfurt Assembly over their own revolutionary origins. The Hungarians felt that they could legitimately speak for the country and, since the reforms came through the Diet, acceptance by the nobility as well as the people was assured.

Concern over legality was also a source of serious weakness. The Diet, even with both Houses in agreement, could not impose its will on the King. No bill passed by the Diet could become law without royal consent. Furthermore, the Diet had no legal basis to force the King to take action and neither did it have the means. Not a single soldier was under the command of the Diet.

For the foregoing reasons, the revolution under radical leadership in Budapest becomes crucial to the success of the Diet. The Committee of Public Safety did not have the moral and legal authority of the Diet but its power was based on an armed force and actual or potential support from and influence over the entire country.

The fears of a bloody uprising, communicated to the Court by the Palatine and many royal advisors, probably had more weight with the Court than the most carefully-delivered speech in the Diet. Thus, the power of the radicals in Budapest forced the King to accept the relatively moderate demands of the Diet as the lesser evil.

A parallel with the events in France in July 1789 offers itself here. Just as the destruction of the Bastille and the popular revolution in Paris saved the French National Assembly and enabled it to proceed with the needed reforms, so did the revolutionary activity in Budapest sway the Court to cooperate with the Diet in order to avert the greater dangers inherent in a revolutionary Budapest. Petőfi, Jókai, Vasvári, Irányi and their fellow radicals in the Committee of Public Safety, together with the aroused citizens of Budapest, emerged as a major factor in the successful transformation of the country.

While the radical revolutionaries presented the "greater danger" to the Crown, their challenge to the authority of the Diet was also of great consequence. Without this challenge, the Diet would have undoubtedly moved more slowly and granted less. Applying the same principle of power described in relation to the Vienna Court, one might say that the internal conditions were affected by the radicals' threat to push aside the Diet members if the deputies did not pursue a more liberal mode of action.

In the final analysis, it appears that both externally and internally, the radicals were indispensable to the victory of the revolution and that their influence waned after its goals had been accomplished by mid-April.

# CHAPTER VII
# TEMPORARY LOSS OF DIRECTION OF THE RADICALS AND THEIR ATTITUDE TOWARD THE WORKING CLASS AND THE PEASANTRY

The establishment of the Batthyány Government in the capital and the dissolution of the Committee of Public Safety reflected a change in the political situation. The radicals lost their instrument of power and, for the moment at least, posed no serious challenge to the new Government. It appeared that the Government had the confidence and support of many Hungarians and even the radicals did not deny this. Vasvári wrote in a newspaper article:

> "At first, every region of the country joined with us, [the radicals], in general sympathy. Pest became the leader. The nation watched every step we made and followed us faithfully. But in its leadership role the youth of Pest went too far ahead. The masses were not able to follow. They lost sight of the leader over the horizon. Thus, the youth of Pest and the nation lost sight of one another."[1]

The division of the young radical intellectuals from the rest of the country was particularly well-illustrated by the public's reaction to the anti-royalism of the radicals. Petőfi's poem "To the Kings" with its refrain,

> "No matter what impudent flatteres say,
> There is no *beloved* King any more."

became known throughout Hungary within a few days and met with a very unfavorable response. Newspapers in every region denounced Petőfi as a traitor and inferior literary talents wrote replies such as:

> "No matter what the immature Petőfi says,
> The beloved King lives above us."[2]

In faraway Transylvania, the Petőfi poem was banned by the authorities.[3] It even found its way to the Court and King Ferdinand demanded that legal proceedings be taken against the poet.[4]

The young radicals of the March days also seemed to have lost their sense of direction. According to Vasvári, some of them such as Bulyovszky and Degré, became governmental officials. Some returned to their former occupations to "wait for better times" and others demonstrated their love of country by joining the National Guard.[5] Jókai became the editor of a literary magazine and he made Petőfi associate editor. Vasvári tried, unsuccessfully, to obtain a teaching position at the University of Budapest.[6]

Budapest did not become quiet at once. As there no longer were constructive outlets for the citizens' pent-up emotions, a certain segment of the population turned in a negative direction. The *March Fifteenth* saw as a "sad sign of disease" when a public meeting before the National Museum demanded that Jews should be thrown out of the National Guard and denied residence in the inner city.[7] Unfortunately, the anti-Jewish sentiments[8] did not stop at public demands. On April 19 the capital witnessed an anti-Semitic riot. The "lower classes of the people armed with sticks, knives and axes" turned against the Jews in the inner city and committed atrocities. "It was their purpose to expel the Jews from the city *via facti.*"[9] There were no reports of deaths but there were numerous wounded.

Since there were similar incidents in the countryside, the Government reacted to the riots energetically. A ministerial decree, signed by all the Cabinet members, ordered criminal proceedings be brought against those taking part in the "violation of security of the person and property of peaceful citizens," and warned that any future gathering aimed at disturbing the peace would be dispersed by armed force. The decree also specified that no one could call popular meetings without first stating the purpose and place to the authorities.[10]

It is interesting that none of the radicals objected to this limitation of the freedom of assembly. Their anger uniformly turned on those who had committed the outrages. The editor of the *March Fifteenth*, Pálffy, wrote that scenes like those witnessed on April 19 in Budapest "defile this decent and outstanding city" and that he would like to erase that day from the city's history.[11] Two days later, the popular actor, Egressy, wrote an indignant article in the same paper separating the revolution from anti-Semitism: "Our revolution is respectable because the revolution not only regarded person and property as inviolably sacred, but made it secure by law." Egressy claimed that the anti-Semitic riot had been a "counterrevolutionary attempt of the overthrown regimé which used the dregs of the people" to accomplish its purposes. The "dregs" were:

> "Partly those who are stupid or worthless enough to allow themselves to be bribed and used as the blind tools of the overthrown regime; partly those who are robbers and thieves. No one should dishonor the class of young artisans by adding them to that group [mentioned above]. But every class has its bottom; if there are some [artisans] among those who took part in this transgression, it is certain that they are not highly regarded by the better element among the young artisans themselves."[12]

There is no evidence that the anti-Semitic disturbances were instigated by the "overthrown regime," and Egressy did not substantiate his accusation in his article. It is true, however, that incidents of this kind brought disrepute to the revolution.

What is interesting about the radical actor's comments is his defense of the "young artisans." The other members of the radical intelligentsia fully shared his views. They had great sympathy and understanding for the working man but they did not have much contact with him. With the exception of Vasvári, who tried to educate the workers and lectured to them on Cabet's utopian socialist views,[13] their contact was scarce, indeed.

The radicals'attitude toward the workers tended to be idealized and abstract. Petőfi wrote some beautiful lines on how only the poor really loved their country and made the greatest sacrifices for a fatherland which gave them nothing in return.[14] But, this sympathy and understanding never led to a concern for the special interests of the workers or, after the liberation of the serfs, for those of the peasants.

Lack of identification with the working class and unwillingness to provide leadership for the satisfaction of specific demands were characteristic of the radicals even during the most heated days of the revolution. Vasvári publicly recounted that he and his friends from the Hall of Liberty (Pilvax Café) had been approached by a few youthful artisans. The young artisans, sent in the name of 4,000 more, asked the radicals to lead the workers and to be their spokesmen. Citing the principle of equality stated in the Twelve Points, the workers called upon Vasvári and his colleagues to lead them in capturing the "chest of the guilds" and to "burn the tyrannical guild laws which are kept in the chest at the Square of Liberty.[11]

The journeymen, (it seems certain that Vasvári was referring to them when he says "young artisans"), understood the meaning of equality in the Twelve Points diffferently from Vasvári and his friends. The guild laws prevented many journeymen from improving their conditions. What they were asking was equality of opportunity: the chance to become independent craftsmen without spending long years in inferior status and to join the guilds without payment of high entrance fees. The journeymen were asking the radicals to help their cause by using the same means the radicals had used to gain their ends: direct popular action.

Vasvári was unwilling to help the journeymen. After listening to their entreaties and talk of violence, he decided that they should be kept in reserve for the "second act of the revolution, if it should come." For this second act, he and his friends had "two bloody plans" which they would pursue if Radetzky decided to move against Hungary. "We have to be ready for anything, because the Austrian Cabinet has no conscience, honor or loyalty. . .it wants to play its evil role to the last scene which will come soon and we shall be able to applaud."[16]

Apart from foreseeing future trouble with Austria when very few others expected it,[17] Vasvári formulated his ideas in regard to the working class quite clearly. He, the radical revolutionary, planned to use the desperate conditions of the workers to further his own cause, the cause of national freedom. He was not willing to give them leadership in their cause, in spite of his sympathy for the workers. Instead of agreeing to help them solve their problems by employing direct popular action, Vasvári recommended that they use legal means. "I propose that . . . the grievances of the artisans be redressed by the Government."[18]

Vasvári's attitude was typical of other radical intellectuals. They all clearly separated themselves from the workers' cause or they ignored it. We know of only one, a lawyer named Kecskés, who gave the workers complete support. On April 22, posters appeared with his signature demanding bread for the people, abolition of the guilds, fixing the price of food, expropriation of Church property and land distribution among the peasants.[19] There must have been other demands, however, as Degré mentions in his memoirs that at a public meeting someone advocated general redistribution of all property and caused a panic among the property-owning city burghers. According to Degré, those who advocated such views were "immoral and of obscure background" and dangerous. He praised Nyári effusively for quashing these proposals at the meeting.[20]

It is very telling that there were no reports in the April and May issues of the *March Fifteenth* of labor strikes or wage demands. This is rather surprising as journeymen in Budapest initiated several strike movements at that time to improve wages and hours.[21] The silence about these labor problems indicates Pálffy's lack of concern with the problems of the working class.

This attitude toward the workers must have weakened the position of the radicals, as they were in need of support from some social stratum if they hoped to remain a political power in Hungary, or even in Budapest. Of the capital's population of approximately 160,000, there were about 10,000 day laborers, 8,000 journeymen and a bare thousand factory workers.[22] Although this group lacked the property qualifications to vote, they could have been most easily mobilized for revolutionary action. If Vasvári, Petőfi and their friends desired a "second act," closer contact with the workers would have been indispensable.

This is especially true in light of the fact that the radicals did not like the urban bourgeoisie, whom they derisively called "timid shopkeepers." The radical intellectuals did have the support of many from the intelligentsia, the professional class, civil servants, clerks and, of course, the university students. But their numbers were few in relation to the rest of the population.

The political future of the radicals was dependent, in part, upon achieving national significance. Thus, the radicals would have been greatly strengthened if they had gained the support of the peasantry.

As a class, the peasants had gained the most from the April Laws, but they still had grievances and further demands. Before 1848, the Hungarian peasantry fell into two major groups.[23] In the first group were those who owned a "plot" which was subject to feudal obligations. The peasant had to give two or three days of free labor weekly, as well as a certain percentage of his produce, to the nobleman of his village. There were 624,000 families, (excluding Transylvania), in this group. They derived the most from the April Laws because they were relieved of their feudal burdens and received clear title to the land they held.

The second and more numerous group, about 914,000 families, (excluding Transylvania), did not own their land. These "cottagers" worked as laborers on the noble's estate on a contract basis. The life of the cottager changed only in a legal sense. He became a free man but had to continue working on the land of the noble on a contract basis as before. If he rented land, he continued to pay the same rent to the noble.

This rent was most often paid in kind, which meant labor services and a certain portion of the gross product. What the landless cottager owed to the noble proprietor was very similar to what the "plot" owner had had to give before the April Laws.

Many of the landless cottagers found it difficult to comprehend the legal distinction existing between them and the peasants who had held title to some land previously. It appeared unjust to many of them that the April Laws did not rid them equally of their bonds. A serious source of potential unrest existed among these peasants which could have been utilized by the radicals.

There were still even more obvious grievances. The peasant had to continue to give a certain percentage of the produce of his vineyard to the nobleman of his village. The nobles had retained their hunting and fishing rights, the right to maintain taverns, mills, local butcher shops and to levy tolls at market places.[24] These remnants of feudalism had little cash value, but they were still a source of annoyance. The situation in Hungary, after the liberation of the serfs, was in many respects analogous to that in France before the 1789 revolution.[25]

Considerable unrest accompanied the changes which were underway. There were hundreds of incidents all over Hungary. Sometimes peasants refused payment to the nobles; often they took land belonging to the nobles and began to cultivate it. There were many cases of peasants forcibly retaking property which had been usurped from the village communities during decades of enclosure. In some places, the peasants took over forests or grazing land belonging to the nobles and were restrained only by the regular army.[26] The seriousness of the situation is best illustrated by the fact that the Government declared martial law against those who did not respect law and order and private property.

What was the position of the radical intellectuals in this situation? Previously, Petőfi had assumed the role of peasant leader and had threatened the nobility with a peasant war. However, this he did only to bring about the abolition of serfdom. Even his notorious poem "Glorious Great Lords" contained the idea that the country was in need of both nobility and peasantry and that the peasants should move against the nobles only in the event they were denied freedom.

Petőfi, Jókai, Vasvári and their colleagues thought the peasants had gained enough with their freedom granted through the April Laws. Vasvári wrote that the most important immediate tasks of the country were the maintenance of peace between social classes and the enlightenment of the peasant masses about the benefits of the new law.[27] Other radicals reacted similarly. The journal edited jointly by Jókai and Petőfi had articles about the peasantry saying that the peasant had no idea of fatherland, did not even know the national colors and was not grateful for the freedom which had been given to him. The peasants "hate the man who wears a jacket and have no trust in him . . . they do not take up arms, nor believe our words nor assist our plans. Thus, God punishes us for the crimes of our fathers."[28]

Possibly, the radical intellectuals took this position toward the peasantry because they were from the gentry themselves and despite their radicalism, they still had close personal ties with the nobility.[29] But, revolutionary intellectuals quite often cross "class barriers" if the cause of the revolution demands it. It was the task of Vasvári, Petöfi, Pálffy and the other radicals to represent the cause of the revolution in Hungary more consistently than any other group or party. Modernization of Hungary and national independence were the two major goals of that revolution. No revolutionary fighting for these causes could promote the demands of the peasantry which were, in part, against private property. On the other hand, peace between the classes had to be maintained or national unity would have been sacrificed. National unity was necessary for national independence in the face of the challenge which was expected from Vienna. Thus, the radical intellectuals, as revolutionary patriots, followed the inner logic of the situation by not identifying themselves with the demands of any particular social class.

From the point of view of political expediency, this was not a very wise course because, in turn, no particular class identified itself with the radical intellectuals either. All that can be said for the action of the radicals is that it was consistent.

The stand taken by the radical intellectuals was not the only possible course. There was at least one example of a different sort of "leftism": the course followed by Mihály Táncsics, the political prisoner liberated by the revolution on March 15. About two weeks after his release, Tancsics began publication of a weekly called *Munkások Ujsága,* the *Workers' Newspaper*; which was directed primarily to the peasants. Its purpose was, as Táncsics put it in his memoirs, "to explain to the little-learned multitude what is indispensable for them to know."[30]

In his paper, Tánicsics developed and propagated a political program which was unique in the spring of 1848. Immediately after the April Laws were announced, he strongly urged universal suffrage declaring it a "crime against nature" to deprive anyone of his voting rights because of lack of property or religion."[31] Representing the special interests of the peasants, Táncsics demanded the elimination of the remaining feudal burdens and the abolition of contractual arrangements between the nobles and cottagers which in practice perpetuated the peasants' servitude. In this context he wished to compensate only those nobles whose annual income was less than 3,000 florins.[32]

Private property seemed even less sacred to him when he proposed that church lands be sold and the state pay the salaries of the clergy. Suggesting land redistribution even more directly, he asked that estates belonging to traitors be "given to the landless Hungarian peasants and brave volunteer soldiers."[33]

Táncsics also displayed great sympathy for the urban working class. While the *March Fifteenth* reported very little about the workers' movement in the capital, Táncsics' weekly published the demands made by the printers in May and he supported them in their struggle for higher wages and better working conditions.[34] Táncsics also spoke out on behalf of the the printers at public meetings and for his help, as he put it, he was given the title "father of the printers."[35]

He greatly damaged his public image, however, by proposing that all titles be abolished.[36] Wishing to emphasize equality, he insisted that everyone be addressed with the form the peasants used toward one another. In highly class-conscious Hungary, this proposal never found public acceptance. Since Táncsics returned to the theme of titles many times during 1848, his name became associated with this question so much so that most politicians considered him to be something of an eccentric.

Although a lone fighter, he had considerable influence among the peasantry with whom he completely identified. His paper had less than 900 subscribers but it was printed in 6,000 copies and distributed free to the peasants on market days.[37] While most of the radical intellectuals failed, Táncsics with his program gained enough followers to be elected in several electoral districts to the first representative assembly.

# CHAPTER VIII
# THE BEGINNING OF RADICAL OPPOSITION TO THE RESPONSIBLE NATIONAL GOVERNMENT IN BUDAPEST

The latter part of April and early May was a period of withdrawal for the radical intellectuals. They used this time to clarify their ideas on radicalism and regroup their forces. Their attitude toward the Batthyány Cabinet was best summarized by the *March Fifteenth*: "We are prepared either to praise them or disparage them. If there is something worth praising, we will be glad to do it. But, if there is something to disparage, that will be even easier."[1] The records show that the paper found much more to criticize than to praise.

Apart from a condescending remark which granted the Cabinet's integrity,[2] there was nothing complimentary in the paper during the ensuing weeks. There was, instead, a great deal of hostile criticism on a wide variety of issues. To begin with, Pálffy questioned the origins of the Government's power. The "ministers were only the products of a few county campaign managers and the landed aristocracy," wrote Pálffy. If the Cabinet did not call for a parliament immediately, it would prove that it was afraid of the people. Then, the Cabinet ministers did not deserve to hold their offices for even an hour.[3]

With reference to Kossuth's threat to suppress the revolution in the capital if it arrogated national powers, Pálffy quoted from a contemporary French paper, *La Réforme,* ". . . nine tenths of the Hungarian nation would not have believed yesterday that such words could come from the lips of Kossuth. . . . We have known for a long time that Mr. Kossuth does not always possess determination but even we did not think him capable of making such an anti-liberal statement."[4]

The radicals criticized the Government for retaining conservative bureaucrats from the previous administration.[5] The strongest attack, however, was made against the Cabinet's lack of decisiveness in clarifying Hungary's relationship with Austria. "Two candles stand before you. You lit one for the honor of the nation; the other for the pacification of the Vienna Government. We ask you to extinguish one of them. You choose the one, please."[6]

A few days later the paper warned that the country was on the verge of a struggle and was as little prepared as the country had been before the catastrope at Mohács. The nature of the coming struggle was spelled out: "The war with Austria is as certian as two and two are four."[7] The *March Fifteenth* expressed bitterness at the lack of preparation of the Government: "Its behavior is similar to that of a person whose house was set on fire at night; instead of putting on a warm coat and quickly leaving, he sits down at a dressing table to comb his hair and dresses as if he were going to a ball."[8]

The radicals correctly pointed to the need for clarification of the relationship with Austria as the most vital problem of the new Government. The Court had agreed to an independent and responsible Hungarian Cabinet, but had left certain aspects of the relationship open to "negotiation." This was especially the case for the Ministries of Finance, War and Foreign Affairs which had previously been directed from Vienna for the entire Habsburg Monarchy. There was no separate Hungarian diplomatic service, no Hungarian army and no Hungarian currency.

There were Hungarian regiments in the Imperial-Royal Army, but they were not kept in Hungary. The garrisons in Hungary were, for the most part, manned by Austrians, Italians and other non-Magyar troops whose loyalty was to the Habsburg Emperor alone. Even the new War Minister, Colonel Mészáros, was out of the country at the time of his appointment. He was serving under Radetzky in Italy and was ordered to return to Hungary only on May 7.[9]

Fiscal matters did not look promising either. Kossuth, the Minister of Finance, inherited a nearly-empty treasury. The coins and banknotes in circulation had been issued in Vienna for the Empire; now, a Hungarian monetary system had to be established. In addition, King Ferdinand had made it plain on April 7 that he expected Hungary to assume one fourth of the Imperial state debt, which would have meant a yearly expenditure of 10 million forints out of an approximate total state revenue of 30 million.[10]

So, the problems facing the Government were grave and the radicals were in the position of all opposition parties: they could levy criticism freely and were not responsible for the affairs of the state.

In addition to criticism, there seemed to have been a sincere effort on their part to clarify the idea of radicalism for themselves and the public. Indeed, who was or was not a radical was very much open to argument in those days. Former conservatives regarded even Batthyány a radical: actually, Batthyány was a liberal monarchist willing to go to almost any length to reach an accommodation with Austria. Széchenyi considered his fellow cabinet member, Kossuth, a radical.

Pálffy read references to the Hungarian Cabinet as a government of radicals in the *London Times*.[11] At this point, Pálffy found it necessary to give his own definition of a radical. "The first and most important characteristic of the radical party[12] is that it does not recognize existing historic rights when it wishes to put its ideas into practice in the legislature. It considers only what is useful and profitable for the country. Before the radicals, there is always a *tabula rasa*."[13] At a later date he wrote, "This party is nothing but the [manifestation of the] spirit of the period. It is the young revolutionary party which carries the flag everywhere in Europe. It is this party that is completely dissatisfied with the policy of the cabinet."[14]

Táncsics' explanation of radicalism was presented to the peasants as the only way to improve conditions. The radicals would take new, just and good measures irrespective of the past.[15]

The radicals also made an attempt during this period to create a formal organization. The young men meeting in their cafe, the Hall of Liberty, reorganized their forces a few weeks after the dissolution of the Committee of Public Safety. On May 8, 1848, they formed an association and called it the "March Club." According to their charter, their foundation was upon the principles of the Twelve Points. They wished to develop and spread the principle of liberty and would seek to bring about liberty through discussion, debate and any other means the membership would decide upon.[16]

Apparently, the membership was more inclined to action than to discussion because with the establishment of the March Club, there was a renewal of revolutionary activity in the capital.

## CHAPTER IX

## RENEWED REVOLUTIONARY ACTIVITY IN MAY AND JUNE AND ELECTIONS TO THE FIRST REPRESENTATIVE ASSEMBLY

### A. *Demonstrations against the military and campaigns against the Government.*

Two days after the press had informed the public of the formation of the March Club, the capital witnessed a hostile demonstration by a large crowd in Buda against the commandant of the Buda garrison, Baron Lederer. Lederer had become extremely unpopular during the previous weeks because it was known that, under false pretexts, he had prevented the Committee of Public Safety from obtaining enough arms in March.

It was customary in those days for groups to express their dislike by giving a sort of mock serenade under the windows of the public figure they wanted to ridicule. This was the intention of about one hundred youths carrying only drums and other noise makers on the evening of May 10 when they arrived at Lederer's residence accompanied by a considerable crowd.

The military had made preparations to receive the crowd. Infantry was hidden inside Lederer's home and neighboring buildings and the cavalry was held in readiness. As soon as the serenade began the lights went out in the General's house. At this signal soldiers with fixed bayonets attacked and cavalry with drawn swords charged the demonstrators. No warning was given, no request made that they disperse. About 20 persons were seriously injured and many others suffered minor wounds. Order was quickly re-established.[1]

This gross over-reaction by the military provided the *March Fifteenth* with a convenient opportunity to denounce the Batthyány Cabinet as completely powerless and to call for its resignation: "It is our wish that Pál Nyári should form a new cabinet. There should be unity with Kossuth. All doctrinaire questions should be set aside. We need brave and determined men who can act."[2] To this Degré added the following personal call: "If that is how things are, fellow citizens, let us rearm ourselves because there are enemies around us, unchivalrous, cowardly enemies. At least, we should not die with empty hands."

The outrage felt by the radicals was shared by many. On May 12, Petőfi called a large public meeting to be held on the square in front of the Museum at which he was the principal speaker. As he admitted later, "I shouted to the people in a mad rage that I would not trust my dog, not to mention the country, to the cabinet."[3] Degré, Táncsics and Pálffy also attended.

Petőfi recommended three specific demands be made to the Cabinet and the royal plentipotentiary, Archduke Stephen. 1. The representative assembly be called as soon as possible. 2. A special commission including radicals be formed to investigate the responsibility for the military atrocities. 3. The soldiers who had committed the crimes be punished.[4] These suggestions were accepted by the crowd and two delegations were elected. One delegation, headed by Petőfi and including Táncsics, Pálffy and Degré, went to Batthyány's home. The Cabinet, which was in session there, received the delegation at once and the Prime Minister promised that their demands would be satisfied.[5]

Petőfi's demands were most sensible proposals under the circumstances. At this point, an assembly would be the only body to exercise effective control over the Cabinet. Petőfi also had every expectation of being one of those to exercise this control. Urging an early assembly meeting had been a consistent policy of the *March Fifteenth* since April 18.[6]

Although in the Lederer incident the radical intellectuals appear as petitioners rather than decision makers as they had been in March, it still should be regarded as a turning point. Petőfi and his friends were once again accepted as popular leaders and were able to bring direct pressure on the Cabinet. Five days after the meeting at Batthyány's home the Government issued a proclamation setting the date for the opening of the assembly for July 2, 1848.[7]

B. *Reaction in the countryside.*

With the up-coming elections, the attitude of the country toward the radicals became crucial. In March, Petőfi and his friends had received popular support but the support was given primarily against the Vienna Court. In May, support of the radicals would have meant the repudiation of some of the most popular and respected national leaders, Batthyány, Deák and, above everyone else, Kossuth. The odds were against the radicals.

In fact, there were very unfavorable reactions in many parts of the country to radical critricisms of the Cabinet. In provincial towns and county assemblies, the politics of the *March Fifteenth* were denounced and the Cabinet was given assurances of the people's support.[8] These demonstrations of loyalty to the Cabinet, initiated as a rule by the mayor or some member of the country nobility, were apparently expressions of the sentiments prevailing among the ruling class. One of the more interesting pro-government resolutions came from Heves county in central Hungary: "[In Heves county] they declared that they would not listen to a proletarian club and a few unruly literati rebels and would not allow some little writers in Pest influence the country."[9] Some of the speakers in Heves county accused the youth of Pest of being republican extremists; others accused Pálffy of being a Russian or Austrian spy. An outraged speaker even urged that 2,000 muskets be obtained from the Government and the people from Heves go to the capital and get rid of the radicals.

Although such extreme views did not find adherents, many counties sent deputations to Budapest carrying assurances of support from the provinces. It was an indication of the changing climate of opinion. A few weeks earlier, the Committee of Public Safety had received such greetings. Now, the support was being given to the Cabinet. The radicals could have countered these expressions of solidarity to the Cabinet only by appealing directly to the peasants and by-passing those who made public opinion in the provinces: the city magistrates and country nobles. The radicals were either unwilling or unable to do this. Under these circumstances, the coming national elections did not hold much promise of success for them.

C. *The elections to the first responsible assembly and the defeat of the radicals.*

At the coming election about one half of the adult male population had the right to vote. Excluded were those who owned less than about 10 acres of land or other property with a value less than 300 forints.[10] Artisans, merchants and factory owners were included if they had at least one employee and so were all professionals and clergymen regardless of their income. The minimum age for voting was 20 and for candidacy for public office was 24.[11]

These voting requirements served to exclude the landless peasants, cottagers, journeymen and city workers. It also prevented some of the young intellectuals from running for a seat in the assembly because they were not yet 24. (This was the case for Vasvári and Jókai, for example.)

Petőfi, Táncsics, Irinyi and Irányi all ran for seats in the new assembly, but the radical intelligentsia did not produce enough candidates to constitute a serious challenge to the entrenched political forces in the country.

The *March Fifteenth* conducted a poor electoral campaign for the radicals. A few weeks before the election an article in the paper stated that the radicals had no illusions of success. They did not have the means necessary "to make politics" and their only hope was that a "manly" party would be formed among the deputies to whom the love of freedom would give strength.[12] Similarly, the paper wrote on June 8, "The truly national party will remain a pitiful minority. Until now, the people wished to serve the noble gentlemen. Now the people will be used to admire the gentlemen's political wisdom."[13]

Petőfi, running for office in his home town in central Hungary, hoped to champion the radical cause in the assembly. There was no more faithful friend of the people in Hungary in 1848 than Petőfi. He could rightly expect to become one of the nation's representatives.

However, his poem "To the Kings," and his known republicanism had made him very unpopular in a country where—as the *March Fifteenth* expressed it—"Royalism was almost a religion."[14] Petőfi was realistic enough to see that his anti-royalism and violent opposition to the Government would hurt his chances, so, before the elections, he made a half-hearted attempt to minimize his previous anti-Government prononuncements. In the journal he edited with Jókai, he published an article in early June stating that in his declaration of no confidence in the Cabinet he had not wanted "to drive them away," but rather to encourage the government to behave in such a way that it would gain general confidence and love.[15] A statement such as this cannot be regarded as a wery strong declaration of loyalty, but even this he found difficult to let stand. He hastened to add a few lines saying that no matter how great the ministers were, he believed as the great French Revolution did, that there were many useful men in the state but that no one was indispensable.

Explanations of this nature did little to endear Petőfi to pro-government public opinion. Neither were his attempts to explain away his republicanism very convincing:

> "As for my poem "To the Kings," which is the chief cause of my unpopularity, it was the first open voice of republicanism in Hungary. Those who believe that it will be the last are very wrong. Monarchy is coming to an end everywhere in Europe: not even omnipotent God can save it any longer. If an idea becomes universal, the world will be destroyed before one can erase the idea. Such is the strength of the idea of republicanism now. . . . But the monarchy still has some future with us, and we unquestionably need it at the present. Therefore, I did not declare a republic, (as they accuse me), I only touched upon the idea in order to familiarize us with it."[16]

Petőfi's reasoning was very similar to the line of the *March Fifteenth.* Csernátoni pointed out that he considered the democratic republic the most perfect form of government and the final goal of Hungary. For the time being, however, the country could stand only as a monarchy, and as a monarchy under King Ferdinand V, he wrote.[17]

The radicals' ambivalence on the question of the monarchy was only in part a concession to royalist public opinion. There was another element. On May 15, the students and workers marched in the streets of Vienna again, demanding universal suffrage. Ferdinand and the Court granted the wish of the demonstrators but left Vienna after this incident and took refuge in Innsbruck.[18] The Hungarian Government somewhat naively hoped that the Court would exchange the quiet safety of a small Austrian town for a large and potentially rebellious city and invited Ferdinand to come to Budapest.[19] It seems that the invitation had a dual purpose:

First, with the presence of the King in the Hungarian capital, the Government wished to quiet the unrest among the nationalities which had started up in the south and was rapidly spreading. Second, the Government hoped to increase Hungary's prestige by making Budapest the center of the Habsburg Empire. A confidential letter written by Kossuth to the head of the Hungarian diplomatic mission in Frankfurt stated: "*Nous travaillon à déplacer le centre de la Monarchie Autrichienne à Buda.* The King will come this month—and, if God helps, will remain here also. We will have to direct Austrian diplomacy. For this purpose, we sent Batthyány to Innsbruck."[20]

The radicals did not know the details of the Government's policy. They quickly grasped, however, that it would be better for Hungary to have the King-Emperor in Budapest rather than in Innsbruck or Vienna. Even the "extremist" Táncsics demanded in the *Workers' Newspaper* that the King come to Hungary.[21]

The radicals' support for Ferdinand's coming to Budapest is one of the earliest manifestations of their willingness to compromise. Petőfi, Pálffy, Csernátoni and Táncsics would accept the "postponement" of the republic, but some of the other radicals would go even further.

Dániel Irányi, a radical lawyer, went so far as to come out in support of the government during his campaign in one of Budapest's electoral districts. He even told his bourgeois constituents of the necessity to preserve the guilds and that he did not support the emancipation of the Jews. He was against the retention of the Upper House and great estate owners in general, and although he stated that Hungary should become a "monarchy based on democracy," he still compromised on his stand toward the Jews.[22]

Irányi, himself, felt the weakness of his platform and defended it in a long letter which appeared in the *March Fifteenth*.[23] He explained that because of the great antipathy toward the Jews, there was no immediate solution to the problem. He assured everyone that he continued to believe in equality but national unity for the defense of the country took precedence over anything else. "Recognition of human rights is one of my ideals, but my greatest ideal is the fatherland. If it is secure, I can realize my other ideals; if it perishess, together with it everything else will perish."

There was some logic in Irányi's political behavior, especially in view of the growing danger to the national cause. The substance of his argument—the idea that national interests come before particular group interests—was later accepted by many Hungarians, including the radicals. This very subordination of special interests to the national interests enabled Hungary—alone among the nations of Europe in 1848—to take a unified stand in defense of her freedom.

Irányi won his assembly seat, while others, less willing to compromise, were unsuccessful. The defeat of the radical intellectuals at the elections is best illustrated by the fate of Petőfi. Although he had muted his anti-royalism, he still refused to beguile and flatter the voters. He told them that they were far from being excellent people—at least up to that time. In his opinion, before March 15 the whole country had the mentality of servants, and his constituency was no exception.[24]

The local "intelligentsia" in the district, the magistrates and the Protestant clergyman whose son was Petőfi's rival, succeeded in turning the people against Petőfi. Before election day, the minister provided free food and drink to all. When Petőfi arrived in the town where the balloting was to take place, his opponents would not allow him to speak and a drunken mob almost lynched him. The worst kind of slander was spread about him. The first peasants, casting their votes, were told by the local gentry that Petőfi was a "rabble-rousing traitor" and a "Russian spy" and that the government would take it kindly if he was defeated or was even beaten. Petőfi was forced to leave town under the protection of armed National Guards who also prevented him from joining with some of his supporters. And even the few hundred who supported Petőfi despite the slander were forcibly prevented from voting.[25]

Petőfi's case was not the only outrage at the elections. His poet friend, János Arany, who came from the peasantry and was a notary, was also prevented from being elected. The local gentry in Arany's district considered it an insult to the nobility that a peasant might be elected to the assembly. The chief county administrator instructed all officials to vote for Arany's opponent. Even some of Arany's fellow notaries were of the opinion that a person better than "just one of us" should represent them. On election day, his supporters were waiting in a tight group at 6:00 a.m., ready to vote. They were informed at 1:00 p.m. to return at 3:00 if they wished to vote. However, they became tired of the whole affair and went home.

The disorder accompanying Petőfi's bid for election and the trick played on Arany's supporters were not isolated incidents. There were several occasions of violence as the verification of the mandates indicated after the assembly had convened.[26]

There is no evidence, however, to show that the great majority of deputies was elected improperly. The results were disastrous for the radical intellectuals. Only two of them, Dániel Irányi and József Irinyi received mandates. Táncsics was elected in two districts: his identification with the cause of the peasantry had gained him its confidence.

There were no formal party platforms at the elections. The conservative party disintegrated during the March Days, and a "party line" among the members of the former liberal opposition did not exist. Individuals ran on their own platforms. Most of them shared the beliefs of the former liberal opposition and supported the Cabinet.[27] The representatives in the first Assembly belonged to the following social classes:

Estate-owning country nobility 72%
Urban bourgeoisie 25%
Lower clergy 2%
Peasantry 1%

The bourgeoisie was divided among the following occupations and comprised the following percentages of the total number of deputies:

Independent lawyers 12%
City officials 8%
1% Physicians
Independent merchants and artisans 1%
Other professionals 3%

These statistics[28] indicate that the people voted for their "natural" leaders, the estate-owning nobility. Although feudalism had been legally abolished, the gentry was still in a most powerful position. The future of Hungary was still to be dependent upon the attitudes of the gentry deputies. The political effectiveness of the radicals, on the other hand, would be decided by the pressure they could bring to bear on the Assembly from the outside and how many of the deputies would support the radical causes. There was no way of telling who the radical supporters would be before the actual sessions of the Assembly started.

One of the most pressing problems to face the Assembly was the growing dissatisfaction of the non-Magyar nationalities. By July, dissatisfaction in some parts of the country had led to large-scale violence which threatened the whole future of Hungary.

## CHAPTER X
## THE NATIONALITIES AND THE REVOLUTION

Desire for feedom was characteristic among all the peoples of Europe in 1848. Those who lived under foreign rule desired not only civil liberties but also basic rights as members of linguistic-cultural communities. The non-Magyar nationalities in Hungary were no exception. They followed the example of the Magyars themselves and demanded far-reaching concessions.

Metternich's old rival in Vienna, Count Kolowrat, a faithful servant of the Imperial family, foresaw this development as early as March, and in keeping with the age-old Habsburg principle of *divide et impera,* recommended to the Emperor that the improved position of the Hungarians be counterbalanced by giving support to the non-Magyar claims in Hungary. He strongly urged the appointment of Baron Jellačić to the office of viceroy (*ban*) of Croatia. In Kolowrat's opinion, Jellačić's appointment would be sufficient to offset the action of the Hungarian nationalists.[1]

Kolowrat's recommentdation was accepted, and Ferdinand made the appointment that same day, March 20.[2] Jellačić fulfilled the Count's hopes because the Croats, under Jellačić's leadership, immediately took the offensive in making their own national demands to Budapest.

The Croats had always occupied a privileged position among the various national groups in Hungary. Croatia had been an autonomous province of Hungary for over 700 years, with her own administration and viceroy. The Croats now looked for complete separation from Hungary, but under the Austrian Imperial Crown. They refused to recognize the authority of the Hungarian Government and demanded complete autonomy for their provincial diet and the viceroy, Baron Jellačić. They agreed, however, that military and foreign affairs as well as commercial matters should be handled by the Viennese Government.[3]

The Serbian demands were similar to those of the Croats, with the notable exception that the Serbs could not claim historic precedent since most of them had settled in the southern part of the country at the end of the eighteenth century after fleeing from Turkish rule. The Serbian National Meeting[4] did not want to surrender allegiance to the

Hungarian Crown completely, but they refused to recognize the Hungarian Government and elected their own national leader (*voivoda*) under whose government they wanted to live. They also made themselves independent in church matters by the election of their Orthodox Archbishop, Josif Rajacić, as patriarch.[5] These demands, if accepted, would have meant near autonomy, if not complete separation.

The most numerous nationality group living in Transylavania, the Rumanians, also made their demands. A National Meeting was held in Balázsfalva, (Blaj), on May 15, 1848.[6] In the name of "liberty, equality and fraternity" the assembled group demanded the complete equality of Rumanians with the other nationalities, (i.e., the Magyars), proportional representation in the legislature, free use of their language in the courts and the legislature, and the same rights for the Rumanian Orthodox Church as enjoyed by other churches in Transylvania and the abolition of feudalism.

In the north the Slovaks held a meeting, and under the leadership of two prominent intellectuals, L'udovít Štúr and Jozef Miloslav Hurban, formulated their demands. The Slovaks wished their language to be used in the administration of those counties in which they lived, asked for Slovak schools, and for the use of the Slovak colors along with those of the Hungarian. A plan of what might be regarded the federal reorganization of Hungary also emerged in the Slovak demands.[7]

The demands of these various nationalities all contained certain common features. Above all, the demand for the recognition of their national existence and the wish for autonomy was expressed. They made it absolutely clear that they did not want to be Magyarized. Corresponding to the degree of their political maturity, they wanted to have their ties with the Magyars as loose as possible, but aside from the Croats, who were the most mature politically, none would deny their allegiance to the Hungarian Crown.

All the nationalities emphasized their loyalty to the House of Habsburg, and from the beginning pointedly held their meetings under their own national colors and the Imperial colors jointly. As a rule, they did not turn to the Hungarian Government with their petitions, but went directly to the Emperor in Vienna. It was obvious that they hoped to press their claims against the Magyars with Austrian assistance.

The reaction of the Hungarian Government was hostile. Within the government, one can detect a certain mixture of legal mentality and the following of historical precedents, not surprising on the part of a political élite trained in law. The Government was willing to treat the Croatian problem separately from the start because it could not deny the historic and legal existence—at least theoretically—of the Triune Kingdom of Croatia, Slavonia and Dalmatia. Since the other nationalities could make no historic claims the answer to their demands was always that the abolition of feudalism, freedom of religion, equality before the law and other rights granted under the April Laws, applied to all citizens of Hungary regardless of their mother tongue. While the Government would respect the private use and development of every language, all politicians insisted that the official language should be Hungarian. According to Kossuth "in one country it is impossible to speak in a hundred different languages. There must be one language and in Hungary this must by Hungarian."[8] While Hungarian was declared the official language, the political existence of Slovak, Rumanian, Serbian, etc. nations in Hungary was not recognized either, and measures were taken against several representatives of the various nationalities.

Conditions rapidly deteriorated throughout Hungary, and by the early summer the country was faced with civil war. Excited Serbian peasants in the south and Rumanian peasants in Transylvania attacked their Magyar neighbors and committed atrocities.[9]

Although the Serbian and Rumanian uprisings caused considerable loss of life and property, the main danger seemed to come from Croatia, where Jellačić could rely not only on armed irregulars, but on the Imperial troops under his command as viceroy and Lieutenant Fieldmarshal of the Imperial Army.

Since Jellačić refused to carry out orders from the Palatine or the Hungarian Government and openly aimed at the separation of Croatia from Hungary, the Hungarian Government treated him as a rebel and took steps for his dismissal. Prime Minister Batthyány succeeded in inducing Ferdinand to suspend Jellačić on June 10.[10] But Jellačić continued to enjoy the support of powerful circles in Vienna, including some members of the dynasty.[11] Jellačić did not give up his position, and continued the military preparations against Hungary which culminated in the invasion of the country in September by the Croats.

The Hungarian Government did everything in its power to avoid conflict with Croatia. Several attempts were made to find a solution. The arbitration of a liberal member of the dynasty, Archduke John, was solicited. Since he had become Imperial Regent at Frankfurt, John paid no attention to the affairs of Hungary, but he did arrange a personal meeting between Batthyány and Jellačić.

At this meeting the Croatian leader demanded that military and fiscal affairs of the Habsburg Empire be centralized in Vienna, and that

Hungary take over part of the Imperial debt. To these demands, he added that equality of the Croatian language with Hungarian should be declared and territorial autonomy granted to the Serbs.

After a great deal of talk about unity and the great power status of the Empire, Batthyány tried to channel the discussion to matters directly concerning the relationship between Croatia and Hungary. When Jellačić repeated that there would be no peace until military and fiscal affairs were concentrated in Vienna, the discussion came to a halt without accomplishing anything.[12]

The Hungarian Government made a final attempt to avoid armed conflict at a Cabinet meeting on August 27. It decided that if Croatia were not willing to continue the existing relationship, Hungary would agree to complete separation, wishing only to maintain an alliance with Croatia and to keep the only Hungarian seaport, Fiume.[13] By the end of the summer, however, Jellačić had become the champion of the unity of the Habsburg Empire and, as such, a counterrevolutionary. His troops crossed the frontier of Hungary early in September and a large-scale armed conflict began.

The demands of the various nationalities of Hungary seem quite justified today, and the Budapest Government—apart from its policy toward the Croats—appears to be inconsistent. After all, while it asserted the national rights of the Magyars, it was not willing to grant the same rights to its own subject nationalities. Yet, it would be unrealistic to expect the Hungarian Government to act on the basis of twentieth century concepts in the nineteenth century. The concept of national self-determination had not yet been formulated, similar ideas had little currency even among nineteenth century progressives in general. There can be no question that historically there was a basic difference between the claims of the Magyars and of the other groups. The Magyars had established the state and had maintained it for more than nine centuries. What they were asking for in 1848 was the re-establishment of the full rights of the country: something Hungary had had before the Crown went to the Habsburgs.

The issue was complicated further by the pro-Habsburg sentiments of the nationality groups. On its own terms this was also understandable. If the nationality groups wanted to assert themselves against the Hungarian Government, it was logical that they should try to find support among the adversaries of the Magyars. This led them into alliances with the Court, the Imperial army and bureaucracy, in short with the very forces which stood for the re-establishment of the *status quo ante*. The Court, the bureaucracy and the army welcomed this development. What the nationalities did not realize in 1848 was that a victory of the Court would not free any of them. Croats, Serbs, Slovaks and Rumanians, who ostensibly wanted to be free, actually became counterrevolutionaries by siding with Vienna. After the revolution came to an end, the non-Magyar nationalities received as reward the identical treatment meted out to the Hungarians as punishment: the re-establishment of absolutism from Vienna.

B. *The radical intellectuals and the nationality problem.*

The radical intellectuals approached the nationality question with more sympathy than did the politicians in the Diet or the Cabinet. The radicals' emphasis was not on historic rights, but freedom, which should unite all inhabitants of Hungary. Under the radicals' influence, the Committee of Public Safety issued a manifesto to the Croats on March 31. It was addressed to the "Croats, our beloved brothers," and explained that the purpose of the revolution was not to serve Magyar interests alone but to bring freedom to all the people of the country. Therefore, the cause was common. So was the enemy: the tyrannical Austrian bureaucracy.

In the name of the friendship which had been preserved throughout eight centuries of good and bad fortunes, the radicals asked the Croats not to fight with them. "We, who are one in the interest of common freedom, should forget the difference in language. We should not listen to those who want to rouse us against one another, because they want to use [our] rivalry to weaken and oppress us both."[14]

When the radicals withdrew after Batthyány's Government took over in April, they continued to keep the nationality issue alive, if only through their newspaper, the *March Fifteenth*, which strongly condemned the Government's policy toward Croatia. By not acting, the Government had allowed this "honest people, loving its own nationality so much," to become estranged from Hungary. The *March Fifteenth* suggested Hungary show her friendship toward Croatia with a "magnificent demonstration," and emphasized that opportunities should be provided for the two peoples to get to know each other. As a storm warning to the Cabinet, the paper noted that if nothing were done, the Croatian provincial diet would certainly declare its independence. Then, if the Government tried to subdue the Croats by force of arms, it would appear before Europe in the same light as Austria, fighting the Italians in Lombardy and Venetia.[15] Similarly, Pálffy warned that the Government was wrong to see the Serbian uprising only as the movement of bandits:

> "Which nation, no matter how small, does not want its independence? Which does not want to have a national government and legislature? It is true that the peasants [Serbs] more or less interpret the movement as freedom to rob, and that those who are more educated want to get good land in the Banat. It is true that army officers and Jellačić are reactionaries but underneath all these heterogeneous elements *only one idea can have a future, and this is separation.*"[16] [Italics mine.]

The radicals exposed what they felt were the true causes of the nationality movements, but as they were not in power there was little they could do beyond trying to influence the Government's position and to spread their views through their press. The radicals did attempt to bring about a reconciliation between the Croats and Magyars. A group of young men travelled to Zagreb to demonstrate their friendship. They were very ill-received there and their trip accomplished nothing.[17]

As the spring went on, pro-Croatian manifestations became fewer and fewer and finally disappeared. On June 8, Csernátoni wrote that Jellačić was not fighting for the "holy cause of nationality," but was an exponent of a small clique which wanted to take advantage of the situation for its own selfish ends.[18] A few days later the *March Fifteenth* described the Illyrian movement merely as a "reaction against the victory of Hungarian constitutionalism."[19]

The *March Fifteenth* still had not given up, though. Failing with the Slavs, the newspaper attempted to change the public's attitude toward the Rumanians. The Rumanians are "decent, honest, simple, good-hearted people, and if they are treated well one can get along with them,"[20] the readers were told. Later, on July 8, the newspaper declared that among all the peoples living in Hungary, the Magyars would not find truer friends than the Rumanians.

These views did not result from poetic enthusiasm for the Rumanians, but from what Pálffy believed was a realistic analysis: "In regard to nationality, nothing attracts the Rumanians to the Russians. They are a Western race, their real origin is a Roman colony. Their language is beautiful and melodious and, if cultivated, it will become similar to Italian in pleasantness and softness."[21] The article concluded with the suggestion that the Rumanians should be enlightened about the advantages of the freedom which Hungary gave.

Although the radicals approached the problem of the nationalities in a spirit of understanding and with the desire for mutual cooperation, even they were not devoid of nationalistic intolerance. The very article which was trying to convert Hungarian public opinion to the Rumanian cause, included the naive remark that the Rumanians "would consider it an honor to be allowed to become Magyars."

At other times, there were occasional remarks which indicated that even the editor of the most important radical newspaper considered it best to be a Magyar. Petőfi's candidacy in central Hungary was announced in the following grandiloquent style: "[He will be a candidate] among the most decent and original people where our beautiful race has lived for centuries in full strength, unspoiled. Among them, the withering soul of foreign half-breed elements could not take hold. . ."[22]

In view that these "most decent and original" people almost lynched their prophet a few days later, the newspaper's chauvinistic boast was particularly ill-conceived! Despite such occasional statements, however, the line of the paper was for cooperation and reconciliation.

Toward the end of the summer, when reconciliation was no longer a possibility because the nationalities had taken up arms against the Hungarian revolution, the *March Fifteenth* dropped this line, but it never preached racial hatred either.

Although the Hungarian Government refused to recognize the national rights of non-Magyar groups, apart from those of the Croats, the Magyars did not attack these peoples. The Hungarians were attacked by Jellačić's troops and by Serbian and Rumanian irregulars. Under the impact of these events, even Petőfi, the advocate of freedom for all peoples, became embittered. He poured out his feelings in a poem "Life or Death."

> "Even had I not been born Hungarian
> I would join with them at this time.
> They are abandoned, the most abandoned
> Among all peoples of the world.
>
> . . . . . . . . . . . . . . . . . . . . . . . . . . . . . . . . . .
>
> You: Serbs, Croats, Germans, Slovaks, Rumanians
> Why do you all ravage the Hungarian?
> We defended you from Turks and Tartars,
> In Hungarian hands glittered the swords.
> We shared with you faithfully,
> If fortune was good to us
> We took over half the burdens
> Which misfortune placed on your shoulders.
>
> . . . . . . . . . . . . . . . . . . . . . . . . . . . . . . . . . .
>
> Be it the way you want it
> [To struggle] for life or death in the fields,
> There shall be no peace until the sun shines not

On one enemy on Hungarian land.
There shall be no peace until the last drop of blood
Shall flow from your bad hearts.
You did not want us as your friends.
Now, you will see us as your judges."[23]

The life and death struggle and the annihilation of the enemy was not merely an outburst of violent nationalism. Petőfi wanted to defend the national cause because it had become one with the cause of the revolution. When Petőfi wrote this poem at the end of September, Jellačić's troops were approaching Budapest, and the only alternative was to submit to military absolutism or to defend the revolutionary capital.

Petőfi was not alone in advocating extreme measures against the nationalities. Táncisics even had a plan to give the land of the exterminated Serbs to landless Magyars.[24] Vasvári put his beliefs to the test by fighting first against the Croats and later against Rumanian irregulars in Transylvania where he died in action.

The extreme measures advocated by Petőfi and the others against the nationalities were quite similar to the terror initiated by Petőfi's heroes, St. Just, Couthon and Robespierre. Indeed, the analogy between Paris threatened by the troops of the Duke of Brunswick and Budapest threatened by the troops of Baron Jellačić offers itself here. Just as Brunswick's victory would have meant the destruction of the revolution, Jellačić was also coming to "restore order," which meant establishing the *status quo ante*. In this context, one could hardly see another solution, short of submission, than that given by the radicals: to oppose counterrevolutionary violence with revolutionary terror.[25]

# CHAPTER XI
# RADICAL ORGANIZATIONS AFTER THE OPENING OF THE REPRESENTATIVE ASSEMBLY

## A. *The political situation in early July.*

On July 5, the representative national Assembly held its first meeting. The tasks of this Assembly were formidable. A new system of state administration based on popular representation had to be established and a new fiscal organization and a tax structure based on equality of taxation had to be devised. The nobles needed compensation for their losses due to the abolition of serfdom and some annoying feudal remnants needed attention.

In view of the Serbian rebellion already underway and the trouble which could be expected from the Croats, the most pressing task was the formation of a Hungarian army. An equally grave problem was Hungary's new relationship with Austria.

The Court had acted with correctness since April, although Ferdinand had attempted to induce Hungary to assume a portion of the Imperial debt. This attempt was dropped after strong adverse reaction from the Hungarians. Once the Croats had made it clear that they did not recognize the Hungarian Government, and wished to sever their ties with Hungary, the King had suspended Jellačić from his post as viceroy and ordered an investigation against him. Strictly speaking, this action was incumbent upon the King. At his coronation, he had solemnly sworn to protect the territorial integrity of Hungary.

After the flight of the Court to Innsbruck, Ferdinand, due to his illness, temporarily withdrew from the direction of the affairs of state and plenipotentiary powers were given to Archdukes John in Austria and Stephen in Hungary. The announcements were publicized through the press.[1]

Armed with the royal authorization, Archduke Stephen opened the Hungarian Assembly in Ferdinand's name. In the Address from the Throne he reiterated that the Monarch disapproved of the Serbian and Croatian separatist movements and the King would defend the laws he had sworn to uphold.[2]

The Court's seeming correctness later proved to be only a screen. Vienna was in the hands of the revolutionaries and Radetzky was on the defensive in Italy: the Court had little recourse. The Hungarian Government reciprocated in an accommodating and loyal fashion with its invitation to Ferdinand to come to Budapest. Certainly, the Government had its own motives, but none among those in positions of leadership had any desire to dissolve the relationship with the House of Habsburg. There is much evidence that the public was very royalist in its sentiments and Prime Minister Batthyány and his Cabinet did all they could to keep these sentiments alive.

Batthyány's coterie was also trying to serve Hungary's interests in its attempts to come to terms with the Court. Batthyány, Deák and Eötvös journeyed repeatedly to Innsbruck and even promised the Court that Hungary would support the Austrian war effort in Italy if the Court would avert the danger presented by Jellačić. The Hungarians even agreed to raise 40,000 new troops for Radetzky's army.[3] These negotiations were not public knowledge but determined to a great extent the order of business for the newly-elected Assembly.

B. *The formation of a radical group in the Assembly.*

While the Assembly was occupied with the verification of the mandates of its members and the formulation of rules of procedure, a group of deputies began meeting together after the Assembly sessions in the great meeting hall of Pest county. The organizer of these meetings was Pál Nyári, one of the deputies representing Pest county who was soon to be the leader of the radical opposition.

By early July about 300 deputies were in the capital attending the regular sessions of the Assembly.[4] Out of this number, approximately 50 replied to Nyári's invitation to discuss the problems between the estate owners and the peasantry.[5] This group of deputies formed the second most significant group of radicals in Hungary.

These parliamentary radicals were very different from the young radical intellectuals around Petőfi and Vasvári. They were not journalists, poets, teachers and students but, as Táncsics remarked in his memoirs, for the most part estate-owning nobles.[6] They came from the patriotic lesser nobility and had belonged to the liberal opposition prior to 1848. Many of them were not newcomers to the political arena having held elective offices before, either as deputies at the Diet or, like Nyári, as officials in the county administrative system.

Among them, László Madarász was one of the most conspicuous figures. At the last meeting of the estates, he had been the first to address the deputies simply as "gentlemen" and not "honorable estates and orders." His brother, József, also a member of the Assembly, was in the forefront of this group along with Mór Perczel. Perczel had taken part in the revolution in Budapest during the March Days, and he was now a deputy as well as a high-ranking official in the Ministry of Interior. Several in this group of parliamentary radicals were from the high aristocracy: Count László Teleki, for instance. Teleki, according to a report of a rather hostile British agent, was "endowed with a certain quantum of talent" but he would not hesitate to adopt any scheme to detach Hungary from the "Imperial domains."[7]

Unlike Petőfi and Vasvári and their friends, these deputies had established positions in Hungarian society. Except for Teleki, they did not have great wealth, but they did own sufficient property to live on the incomes they derived from it. The fact that they belonged to the nobility had helped in their election to the Assembly. These politicians ran on individual radical platforms which demanded further rights for the people. A typical radical program submitted to the electorate urged universal suffrage; it called for the abolition of the Upper House because it was contrary to democratic principles; it demanded expropriation of the vast church estates and a state-financed school system. The program included opposition to corporal punishment, capital punishment and wanted the term of military service reduced from six to four years.[8]

The initial emphasis was on social change. The approximately 50 deputies who met at Nyári's invitation also put a social issue at the center of their discussions. Their conference between July 6-12 was concerned primarily with the problems of completing the liberation of the serfs. On a motion of László Madarász, the radical deputies agreed that the dues peasants were still required to pay the nobles for vineyards should be abolished and the state should compensate the nobles.

The problem of the landless peasants still living on manorial lands was also discussed. The radical deputies agreed that this group should be exempt from labor services and payments in kind and that the nobility should be compensated partly by the state and partly by the peasants themselves. The existing obligations should be converted into monetary payments.[9] The deputies also discussed the problems created by the practice of other feudal obligations.[10]

Attention given to rural questions at the conference indicates that the radical country nobles were more aware of the immediate needs and problems of the peasantry than were the radical intellecutals. The radical deputies were also prepared to promote specific measures to improve the conditions of the peasants. Both the intellectuals in the capital and the nobles from the country realized, however, that if the radicals were to become an effective force in politics, they had to unite. Thus, a new radical club was formed in mid-July which was called the "Society for Equality."

C. *The Society for Equality.*

The new political club was the second organization with this name in the history of Hungary. It was an indication of the growing political maturity of the country that the group brought together in 1848 under this name was composed of both nobles and commoners. In the 1790's, Martinovics planned an organization with this name to be made up of non-noble revolutionaries exclusively.

The initiative for the new club had come from the Madarasz brothers. They were the editors of a small radical paper, *Népelem, (Democracy)*, which began publication at the beginning of July and advocated essentially those views presented in József Madarász's election platform. The Society for Equality was not the first Hungarian revolutionary club in 1848. Petőfi, Jókai, Vasvári and other Budapest intellectuals had their own organization, the March Club, which had organized the demonstration against the commandant of the Budapest garrison leading to military brutality and bloodshed in May. There is no evidence that the March Club continued to function formally, but the young members of this club did meet regularly in the Pilvax through May, June and July. They even extended their influence. Mór Mérey and Zsigmond Rosti, two new members of their circle, established the *Radical Lap, (Radical Newspaper)*, which supported the policies of the *March Fifteenth* in June and early July although it was less energetic in its criticism of the Government than was the *March Fifteenth.*[11]

In the beginning of July, the dormant March Club was replaced by a "Democratic Club" which also met at the Pilvax. Little is known about the Democratic Club which lasted only a few days. In Vasvári's words, it planned to excercise a supervisory role over the legislature and encourage it to act vigorously. It also intended to urge the abolition of existing press laws, to fight obscurantism in the country and to enlighten the people about the blessings of liberty.[12]

The *Radical Newspaper* pressed for the establishment of radical clubs. It suggested a "federation of clubs" which would have its center in Budapest and branches in the provincial cities. According to the paper, the intelligentsia of Budapest should provide leadership by developing and spreading modern ideas and inducing the membership in the provinces to accept these ideas. A highly-centralized club federation could become a powerful factor in the political life of Hungary and would become a "mighty supervisor of the government" in all respects.[13]

The editors of the *Radical Newspaper* viewed the French Jacobin clubs as their models. As other revolutionaries in Europe in 1848, such as the radicals in Baden, they not only derived inspiration from the great French Revolution but they also imitated it in its organizational structure.

Against this background, the Society for Equality came into existence in mid-July. Its program first stated the shortcomings of the revolution to date: the press was still restricted; civil equality was circumscribed by the system of voting rights and class rule. Therefore, the Society for Equality was established in order to accomplish the following:

> "We have united to achieve real, unconditional freedom of the press, exempt from any preliminary security deposits.
> We have united to achieve civil rights unrestricted by any property qualifications.
> We have united to lay siege to and to destroy prejudices which maintain class barriers between human beings and between citizens.
> We have united to bring about the disappearance of hostility based on the existence of different languages; we welcome into our association any citizen irrespective of language, as the cause of freedom is common and can be achieved only through mutual efforts."[14]

This statement of purpose subscribed to both by the radical intellectuals and by the radical deputies went far to clarify the ideological basis of their group. Batthyány, Kossuth and Deák, supported by a majority in the Assembly, represented the status quo which included civil liberties and responsible parliamentary government, the essential requirements of a liberal state.

The radicals, in formulating the program for the Society for Equality, developed a rival doctrine which was expressed in the title of their association. The emphasis on equality was the logical step in a political framework which already promised liberty. It meant universal suffrage and the right of all to participate in decision-making, regardless of wealth or property.

The radicals sensed that the introduction of universal suffrage alone would not suffice to bring about democracy. They recognized the need to combat and remove class prejudice which separated citizen from citizen. More than legislative action, the acceptance of a fellow citizen as one's political equal creates the atmosphere of democracy. Hungary was far from a democracy in 1848 or, for that matter at any time during the nineteenth century. If the radicals' program had succeeded, by introducing universal suffrage and breaking down class barriers, the radicals not only would have changed Hungary into a political democracy but would have guided her away from her caste system which remained one of the major ills of Hungarian society until very recently.[15]

The Society had a well-defined program and could rely on some important members of the Assembly. The radical intellectuals could mobilize the crowds in Budapest if needed. The Madarász brothers merged their paper, *Democracy*, with the *Radical Newspaper*, to create a fairly strong paper called *Nepelem Radical Lap*, the *Radical Democrat*. The first issue of the *Radical Democrat* appeared July 15.[16] There was good reason to believe that the radical democrats, intellectuals and deputies, would exercise a greater influence on the course of events than they had been able to do since the days in March.

D. *The early struggle in the Assembly: The question of national defense.*

The radical deputies began their fight for the advancement of their cause during the debates on the house rules. The Committee that had prepared the rules proposed that admission to the visitors' galleries be restricted to those with entrance tickets and that each deputy be permitted to give out one ticket. László Madarász at once countered with the proposition that everyone be admitted on a first-come, first-serve basis.[17] Most likely, he expected the revolutionary youth organized by Vasvári, Petőfi and their friends to make a helpful audience cheering the radical deputies from the galleries. Others present were also aware, however, that at the diets in Pozsony, groups of law students attending meetings had cheered the opposition speakers, although it was against the rules, and a majority of the deputies quickly defeated the Madarász proposal.[18]

The radicals did no better on questions of the agenda. By July 10, the House had elected its president and other officers and was ready to proceed with regular business. At that point, the deputies were informed that Kossuth would make a proposal the next day on the question of national defense. The President of the Assembly requested that Kossuth's speech be put on the agenda as the first item and that the discussion on the Address from the Throne come second.[19]

The question of order was important. The Government planned to ask the House for authorization to establish a large army. To meet the agreement made with the Court, the Government planned to use 40,000 of the newly-formed troops in Italy, under Radetzky's command, and not in Hungary. In so doing, the Government hoped that the Court would pacify the rebellious Serbs and Croats in exchange. The Government preferred to obtain permission of the House to establish the army prior to considering the controversial issue of sending recruits to Italy, which a regular discussion of the Address would have produced.

Apparently, the radical deputies had advance information on the Government's intentions. Nyári proposed that the Address be the first order of business. Supporting Nyári, Perczel argued that before recruits are authorized by the House, Hungarian army affairs should be completely separated from those of Austria. He wished to make it sure that Hungarian soldiers would not be stationed abroad before voting on new troops.

József Madarász stated that he would vote for soldiers to be used in Hungary's defense, but he would not agree, under any circumstances, to use these soldiers against European freedom.[20] Although the radicals' arguments were sensible and even had custom on their side, the Address was placed on the agenda to follow Kossuth's speech.

Kossuth was, by far, the best speaker amon the Cabinet members, and he was also extremely popular among the deputies. Probably for these reasons he, and not Batthyány, was the spokesman for the Government. This was the case on July 11 and continued as long as the Government was in power.

Kossuth began by warning the deputies of the danger to the fatherland. Then he proceeded to show by careful analysis that the danger was real and immediate coming from the Croat and Serbian insurgents in southern Hungary.

He informed the House that the Austrian Cabinet was threatening to end its neutrality in regard to Croatia because, as Minister of Finance, he had stopped sending money to Jellačić from Budapest. He pointed to the absurdity of a threat which meant that the Austrian Emperor threatened the King of Hungary, i.e., himself, with war. He stressed that against these dangers the country could not expect help from abroad. France and Germany were friendly to Hungary but concerned with their own interests. Hungary could rely only upon herself. Therefore, he asked the House to grant 200,000 soldiers and the necessary funds to protect the country.

In a highly emotional state, Nyári, Kossuth's opponent, rose from his seat and interrupting Kossuth shouted his approval. The rest of the House rose with him, and in an outburst of patriotic fever, Kossuth's request was granted.[21]

The decision of the House to establish a large Hungarian army on July 11 was only the beginning of the controversy over national defense. In a debate over the Address from the Throne, the Government had to bring up the question of military aid to Austria in Italy which led to a major clash between the radicals and the supporters of the Government.

## CHAPTER XII
## AID TO AUSTRIA AGAINST THE ITALIANS: INTERNATIONAL REVOLUTIONARY SOLIDARITY OR A POLICY OF EXIGENCIES

During the summer of 1848, the Austrian Court faced not only a revolution in Vienna but also a full-scale war in Italy. Lombardy and Venetia rose against Habsburg rule in March. The revolutionaries expelled the Austrian forces from Milan and Venice and republics were declared in these cities. In addition, the King of Sardinia, Charles Albert, began an initially successful war against Austria. The Austrian position was so bad that Field Marshal Radetzky was ordered to conclude an armistice even at the cost of giving up Lombardy.[1]

The Italian struggle for freedom met with sympathy in Hungary. The Italians sought actively to keep this sympathy alive and to devolop it into active cooperation. A note from the Provisional Government of Milan to Hungary explained that the common struggle for freedom should unite Hungary and Italy against the Habsburgs, and the two nations, united fraternally, would be invincible against the enemies of their freedom and glory.[2]

The Hungarian Government paid no heed to the Italian request. In a major policy address on July 20, Kossuth told the Assembly that he was sympathetic with the Italians but that one should not be led by personal feelings in politics, which was the "science of exigencies."[3] He insisted that if Hungary supported freedom as a principle, she would have to support the Croatian claims also. Kossuth added that if Hungary expected Austria to be a loyal ally, Hungary had to be loyal in return and had to give Austria assistance against the Sardinian attack. Kossuth then read the minutes of the July 5 Cabinet meeting when the Government had made the decision to give aid in accordance with the Pragmatic Sanction.[4]

The minutes disclosed that aid to Austria had been made contingent upon the restoration of peace and order in Hungary, and upon recognition of Hungary's legal, fiscal and military independence. It was also stated that Hungary would not take part in the suppression of the Lombard-Venetian nation and wanted to assist the King to "conclude a peace. . .consistent with His Majesty's dignity as well as the rights, liberties and fair wishes of the Italian nation."

This policy was directed toward averting a break with Austria. Since Hungarian aid was promised only after conditions had become normal in Hungary, it was not likely that Hungarian levies would appear on Italian battlefields for some time. Still, the Government could not have found an issue more unpopular among the radicals than the sending of troops against the Italians. Fellowship with other peoples struggling for freedom, especially if far away and with no influence on home conditions, characterized the European revolutionaries in 1848 and the Hungarians were no exception.

Petőfi had already written about his dream of dying a hero's death for world freedom in 1846. In the first hours of the revolution in Budapest in front of the printing shop where the Twelve Points had been printed, Vasvári warned that the Austrian Cabinet's strength would lie in its ability to set one people against another. He even cited the Italians because the revolutionary movements of 1848 had started there, and he emphasized that people would realize their desire for freedom only through cooperation.[5]

From the debate which followed Kossuth's speech, it became clear that the radical deputies were in complete agreement with the radical intellectuals on this issue. Their combined attack upon the Government's position was begun by one of the very few radical intellectuals to win a seat, József Irinyi. He said it would be "uncivilized" to intervene in Italy and that the Government would make a grave error to believe that it would gain anything from Hungary by helping the Camarilla. One does not ally oneself with the devil to save virtue and Hungary would lose her national honor and would gain nothing from sending her soldiers to fight the Italians.[6]

The *March Fifteenth* pointed out that if the Hungarians intervened in Italy, Europeans would consider their behavior barbaric, and it warned that the nation did not deserve to survive if it aided Austria against the Italians.[7] In a long front-page article the paper accused the Government of duplicity because on July 11 it had asked for troops for the country's defense and then, just nine days later, it admitted that it wanted to use some of them for "hateful purposes."[8] The paper rejected the idea of intervention in principle and charged the Ministers with being heirs to Metternich's policy.

Other radical papers reacted similarly. The *Radical Democrat* informed its readers with big headlines that Mór Perczel had resigned his high office in the Ministry of Interior because he would not serve in a government which would send mercenaries against a civilized cause.[9] Even Táncsics, who confined himself mostly to the problems of the peasantry, wrote in his *Workers' Newspaper* that the Government's Italian policy was bad and would lead nowhere.[10]

The concerted efforts of the radicals forced the Government to reformulate its position. The task was entrusted to Kossuth, and the document which he submitted to the Assembly on July 21 still promised aid to Austria but offered two new safeguards against the use of Hungarian troops against the Italians. First: Austria should offer autonomy to Lombardy and Venetia along with as many free constitutional institutions as possible in the monarchical state. Second: if this was unacceptable to the Italians, a strategic line should be established as necessary for the security of the Austrian Empire and Austria should agree to the separation of territories below this line and grant free constitutional government to the territories remaining with her. Military aid would be given by Hungary only if the Italians rejected both of these alternatives.[11]

The Government's new position still did not meet with the approval of the radical deputies. They renewed their attack as soon as Kossuth had finished reading. First the Madarász brothers and then Nyári tried delaying tactics, insisting that the statement be printed and circulated before discussion began. Possibly, they hoped to organize demonstrations against the bill in the interim. Perczel, with great emotion, declared it would violate free discussion in the Assembly if the contents of the policy were not available in print.[12]

The Government's spokesmen, Kossuth and Deák, replied that too much publicity would be harmful. Kossuth even said that he would not give out one more word of information and that the confidence of the House in the Government was now the question. He asked the House for a vote of confidence on the basis of the facts presented.

Amid shouts of protest from the left, a large majority of the House rose in consent. Then Kossuth added: "I did not wish and did not want to provoke this scene, but when a minority does not understand loyalty and it accuses the Government of trying to prevent freedom of expression in the House, then my reply to this minority is that they are mere dwarfs."[13] This remark about the "dwarf" minority became a permanent epithet of the radical opposition and was quoted on many occasions. The *March Fifteenth* was prompted to remind Kossuth that he was speaking to his equals in the Assembly, and he should not be carried away by passion in the nation's sanctuary.[14] About the Government's policy, the paper stated that the world had never seen such a *noli metangere* cabinet.[15]

The vote of confidence given to Kossuth did not stop the radical deputies from further attacking the Government's policy. Perczel, Nyári and Teleki all delivered major speeches against intervention in Italy. The radicals' opposition was based, in part, on moral grounds and claimed that the Government was acting against the will of the people and public opinion.[16] The radicals were correct in their assessment of public opinion; aid to Austria against the Italians was unpopular in the country and the recall of Hungarian troops abroad was one of the Twelve Points. But the radicals did not base their arguments solely upon morality.

The radicals argued against intervention on the grounds that it was not in Hungry's interest either. Perczel said that once Austria had quelled the Italian rebellion her armies would turn against Hungary and would restore the pre-March conditions. Emphasizing that the people who wanted freedom had to work together, he said that no nation could be free which would help to oppress other nations.[17]

In his own speech, Teleki admitted with intellectual honesty that he would willingly accept this principle for implementation at home as well as abroad, and would grant the separation of Croatia from Hungary if that was the national will of the Croats.[18]

Nyári introduced a new element in the debate by predicting the fall of reactionary Austria. He stated that it would be in Austria's interest to grant freedom to the Italians, and that the only correct way for Hungary to act was to recognize the territorial independence of the Italian provinces of the Austrian Empire.[19]

History proved these radical deputies to be correct. Their more progressive outlook enabled them to foresee certain consequences to which the Government was blind. But, when the vote was taken the radicals remained a minority, indeed, a "dwarf" minority. The opposition forced the issue to a roll call vote and the results were 36 votes against the Government policy and 233 votes in favor of the principle of sending aid to Austria.[20] Seventy-nine deputies were either absent or abstained.

The action taken by the Hungarian Assembly in regard to intervention provides an excellent example of the lack of cooperation among the revolutionary forces in the various countries. The failure of the 1848 revolutions in Europe was due to this factor to a considerable degree. Although the Hungarian deputies based their policy on the legal responsibilities they believed they owed Austria under the terms of the Pragmatic Sanction, the Vienna Court was not so constrained.

No matter how the Hungarian deputies insisted on legality, the Court was quick to forget legality and to resort to brute force just as soon as it felt strong enough to do so. Thus, history proved the fallacy of the policy of exigencies. It is fortunate for the historical record of the Hungarian revolution that fresh Hungarian troops were never sent to Italy. The mistake in judgment remained only theoretical.

# CHAPTER XIII
# THE INCREASE OF RADICAL STRENGTH IN HUNGARY IN JULY AND AUGUST

Military affairs remained the main political issue in Hungary even after the decision had been made to aid the Austrians. For this, there were three basic reasons. First, while the Assembly was in session rather unsuccessful military operations were in progress in the south against Serbian insurgents. This lack of success was partly due to stiff resistance by the Serbs and partly to the fact that the troops sent to fight them were led by Imperial army officers. These officers, now under the command of the Hungarian Minister of War, were doubtful supporters of the Hungarian cause.[1]

Second, Jellačić remained in open rebellion and continued military preparations in Croatia, constituting a serious threat to Hungary.

Third, it had to be determined whether the new Hungarian army would be organized on the pattern of the Imperial army or on an entirely new, purely Hungarian design.

The organization of the army was delayed purposely by the Cabinet on legal grounds. Batthyány expected that the Austrian army would become integrated with the armed forces of Greater Germany on orders from Frankfurt. As Hungary had never been part of the Holy Roman Empire, Austrian submission to the central German authority would have provided Hungary with legal grounds to establish an independent army of her own.[2]

Batthyány's expectations did not materialize. On August 6, the black, red and gold ribbons symbolizing unified Germany were placed on the regimental flags of the Austrian army. But, on August 7, these ribbons were removed on the order of the Imperial War Minister, Count Latour.[3] Prime Minister Batthyány had sacrificed valuable time and his maneuver was unsuccessful. The question of the organization of the army was placed on the agenda in mid-August.

The Assembly was asked to consider a bill submitted by the War Minister General Mészáros. Mészáros, who had spent his adult life in the Imperial army, did not introduce any major changes in the army organization. His bill would have set up a new method of recruitment based on general conscription.[4] It did not go into such matters as the language of command, colors, insignia and so on. New recruits were to be enlisted into existing regiments, dressed in white frock-like uniforms and to serve under German command and the black and yellow flag.

Mészáros himself realized the absurdity of his bill. He gave an apology explaining that, under the present circumstances, a thorough-going reorganization would take too much time. To establish a new Hungarian army would not strengthen the military power of Hungary, but would, rather, reduce the army to a state of chaos.

These technical arguments were supported by one major political consideration. Mészáros cautiously advanced the idea that the relationship with other parts of the Austrian Empire had to be considered. Hungary should not sever these links completely, because for the most part they were beneficial; only the aberrations of the system need be corrected.[5]

Mészáros could hardly have been more conservative. The *March Fifteenth* summarily called him "Radetzkyan" and a "schwarzgelb Patriarch."[6] Even the Assembly found his bill unsatisfactory. After discussion in committees, a new bill representing a majority opinion was advanced. This version was almost twice as long as that of Mészáros's and specified that new units could be used only in Hungary's self-defense. Regiments already in the field and confronting the enemy should be brought up to full strength with new recruits. All other recruits were to be formed into new regiments. The language of command, flags, colors and uniforms in the new regiments would be Hungarian. As soon as possible, the units already formed would be Magyarized and merged into new regiments.

The new bill empowered the War Minister to name and promote subordinate officers directly, without royal authorization. It prescribed a new oath according to which soldiers would swear allegiance not only to the monarch but also to the Hungarian Constitution, and it reduced the term of military service from six to four years.[7]

The discussion of the organization of the army led to the most heated debate witnessed in the Assembly to that date. There were violent denunciations of the Government, stormy evening sessions, accusations and counter-accusations. The debate continued for a week.[8] Not only did radical deputies violently object to putting new Hungarian recruits in Austrian uniforms, but they were joined by many others who normally gave support to the Government.

The case of the radicals was best presented by Teleki. He saw the real danger not in the lack of soldiers, but in the fact that those military units now existing were not Hungarian in spirit, aims or mentality. In principle, even Jellačić's army was "Hungary's" army, and Teleki demanded that new recruits be enlisted into entirely new, Magyarized regiments. He argued that a completely Hungarian army was the logical consequence of the country's independence, which had been sanctioned by the ruler. He maintained that an army open to talent would more than compensate for the absence of tradition.[9]

Prime Minister Batthyány sensed that the Assembly was closer to the radical viewpoint than it had been at any other time. He urged the deputies to pass a bill which the King would find acceptable; otherwise, it would not become law.[10] On a motion of László Madarász, the Assembly voted to set aside Mészáros's bill. The Committee's bill was then approved in substance. Two alterations were introduced by the radicals which were also approved. Teleki's proposal that in the future only Hungarian-speaking officers should be employed in the army and a proposal by Nyári abolishing flogging were both approved. The measure to abolish flogging was passed only after bitter debates with Mészáros and Széchenyi, who had both wanted its retention.

Even this compromise bill cost the Government a great deal. The roll call vote was 226 deputies supporting the new bill and 117 deputies opposing it.[11] Compared to the meager 36 opposition votes on the Italian question, this was a meaningful gain for the radicals. The *March Fifteenth* jubilantly wrote that 117 deputies were hardly a "dwarf minority."[12]

However, not all the deputies opposed to the bill were radicals. The issue was highly charged. National colors and language meant a great deal in 1848 and some of the new opponents of the Government undoubtedly voted out of patriotic fervor rather than out of well-conceived belief. Still, the vote indicated that the radicals' more determined position could attract votes away from the Government. It remained to be seen if the radicals could force a change in the Government's policy or succeed in detaching Kossuth.

The possibility of Kossuth allying himself with the radicals looked bright during the debate on the army bill. The dissension among the Cabinet members became obvious. Kossuth did not agree with Mészáros's proposed bill and in his speeches he seemed closer to the radicals' position both in tone and substance. During the August 19 session, Kossuth admitted that his views on the army organization differed from those of Mészáros and that he wanted it known that the differences of opinion in the Cabinet had had a "numbing effect" on meetings for days. Essentially, he came out against the bill of the War Minister.[13]

At the Cabinet meetings, Kossuth was supported by Deák and Szemere. Thus, as a result of this issue, a Cabinet crisis seemed in the making and the possibility of a new cabinet under Kossuth's leadership, with the inclusion of the radicals, was present as early as August.

The basis for cooperation between Kossuth and the radicals was the similarity of their views on Hungary's independence. While the Prime Minister always sought a solution agreeable to the King as well as to the nation, Kossuth's prime interest was the nation. On July 29, 18 days prior to the submission of Mészáros's bill to the Assembly, Kossuth wrote in a newspaper article, "As far as the desire of the Austrian government to retain control over our financial and military affairs is concerned, it is my strong conviction that death is preferable to the slightest concession in this respect."[14]

The assertion of Hungarian national rights endeared Kossuth to the radicals. The *March Fifteenth* had been working toward the detachment of Kossuth from his colleagues in the Cabinet for some time. In early May, the paper had written that something really good could be expected only of the Minister of Finance.[15] A month later, it informed its readers that Kossuth did not agree with the vacillating policies of his colleagues in the Cabinet, and said that if Kossuth left the Cabinet, confidence in the remaining ministers would freeze.[16]

Immediately after the publication of Kossuth's article on the army organization, the *March Fifteenth* wrote that Kossuth fulfilled the nation's expectations in him and that the time had come for him "to raise the flag" himself. If he did, the nation would give him unqualified support at once.[17]

The idea that the Cabinet without Kossuth could not exist and would lack a majority in the Assembly was mentioned time and again. On August 4, it was stated that Kossuth could depose his eight colleagues any time, but the eight of them together could not depose him and had to accept him even if they dissagreed with him.[18]

There is no evidence that Kossuth encouraged this campaign but he did not publicly denounce it either. Such a press campaign was certainly helpful in preparing for future cooperation between Kossuth and the radicals, cooperation which became a necessity in the face of the armed attack from Austria.

While the public's attention was focussed on the parliamentary debate concerning national defense, the radical deputies rose to greater political significance than the radical intellectuals who could not participate in the decision-making process. But the radical intellectuals were not passive either. Petőfi still carried his appeals to the nation as a poet. During the late spring and summer, he devoted much of his writing to the political problems of the day.

In a short poem, Petőfi satirized the Court's demands for Hungary's share in the Imperial state debt, and promised that if the Austrian army came to collect, it would be badly beaten and run out of the country.[19] He warned of the dangers threatening Hungary, and urged the Government to act:

"The enemy is getting ready, are we?
What is the Government doing?
Instead of standing guard, it is fast asleep
On the watchtower of the fatherland.
Let us paint our flags black and red
Because mourning and blood
Will be the fate of the Hungarian nation."[20]

Besides his reactions to politics, Petőfi also expressed his view of the future. In a beautiful ode, he paid homage to an idealized personification of the Republic and told of its final victory over the world.[21] In the same spirit, he prophesied that just as Jerusalem had perished, Austria would perish also, and her emperors become homeless outcasts. Their empire was the Calvary of liberty and in their exile, the curses of the oppressed peoples would follow them.[22]

Political poetry was not the only contribution of the radical intellectuals. The *March Fifteenth* and the *Radical Democrat* followed political developments very closely and actively supported the radical deputies. The chances for mobilizing the masses in Budapest to support the radical program decreased somewhat during the summer, because many of the young men had joined the National Guard or had left Budapest for other reasons.[23]

Despite summer vacation at the University, there were a few demonstrations. When the debate on the Italian question was in progress, an assembled crowd tried to force its way into the meeting hall to learn for itself whether the Government really wanted to send soldiers against the Italians. Workers held a meeting to say they would refuse to take up arms against the Italians, and Vasvári led an angry crowd to the Assembly hall protesting the Government's policies.[24]

These were indications that the radical intellectuals had not stopped direct appeals to the people. By the middle of the summer, the real center for radical agitation was the Society for Equality, where the intellectuals and the professional politicans met together and formulated radical policy.

The Society's program was primarily devoted to the need for political and social reforms.[25] However, the Assembly did not discuss these issues during the summer and dealt with only a few of these reforms later. It was not that the deputies were not concerned about the need for further reforms but the pressing problems of national defense had first priority. At that time, the future of the country was dependent upon its military potential.

The radical intellectuals and radical deputies shared a common body of belief and cooperation between them existed from the very start of the Assembly. Often the demands of the radical press and bills presented by radical deputies were almost identical. The *Radical Newspaper*, for example, demanded on June 3 that the Upper House be deprived of its veto power and later it repeatedly came out for the dissolution of that "outdated" legislative body.[26] László Madarász submitted the following bill to the Assembly on July 15: "The so-called 'Upper House' should be abolished as it is an incompatible obstacle to national representation."[27]

Once the Society for Equality began holding regular weekly meetings, under the chairmanship of László Madarász, the cooperation between the radical intellectuals and the radical deputies was strengthened further. The Society began a systematic discussion of the various points of its program. As in March, now again, the freedom of the press was of foremost importance to them.

The radicals had a good case here. There had been no censorship in Hungary since March: however, to establish a newspaper or a printing press, the large sum of five to ten thousand forints was required as a security deposit against possible slander suits. In effect, this law kept the power of the press in the hands of the wealthy. The Society, in a petition to the Assembly, argued forcefully against this requirement. It pointed out that no other profession was forced to pay such large deposits, and that the law treated journalists and writers as morally suspect. The petition criticized the press laws for preventing a writer from freely using his talent and for condemning many writers to the role of mercenaries of big "capitalists."[28] Although the law was clearly discriminatory, the Assembly disregarded the Society's petition.

The Society was more successful, if indirectly, with another issue which appeared on its August 6 agenda. After a lengthy discussion, a resolution was adopted which demanded complete emancipation of the

Jews in the name of natural law, justice and equality. The resolution noted that the Jews had to carry equal burdens with the other inhabitants of the country and that it was absurd to force 400,000 people to suffer "moral slavery" because of their religion: "Representatives, It is your duty to give equal rights to the sons of the same fatherland. It is your duty to put an end to the prejudice of the masses and to bring about justice with the help of legislative power. . . . A nation which tolerates slaves among its ranks is not worthy of the greatest treasure on earth: Liberty. Show that you are worthy of liberty."[29]

This resolution was produced in support of a bill proposing complete emancipation of the Jews, submitted a few days earlier by a noble radical deputy, Ödön Kállay.[30] Although it was a long time before the emancipation bill was put on the Assembly's agenda, the revolutionary period of 1848-49 saw equal rights given to the Jews of Hungary. On July 28, 1849, in one of its last acts, the Assembly granted full and equal rights of citizenship to "every inhabitant of the Mosaic faith who was born in or was legally settled within the boundaries of Hungary."[31]

Members of the Society achieved a partial victory in regard to the abolition of certain feudal remnants also. The conference of radical deputies in early July dealt with these issues. Nyári, László Madarász, Táncsics and others submitted a number of bills to the Assembly in July and August which would eliminate the last vestiges of the feudal system. Nyári proposed that all dues to noble proprietors in kind and in labor services be rendered into money payments. László Madarász recommended the abolition of noble monopolies of hunting and fishing, together with the exclusive rights of the nobles to maintain mills, butcher shops and taverns. Táncsics submitted a bill to abolish the tax in kind on vineyards which the peasants counted among their most serious grievances.[32] In mid-September, when Jellačić was advancing on the capital, the bill on the vineyard tax was brought up by Kossuth and passed.[33]

At the August 13 meeting, a hitherto unknown member, Öttevényi, suggested that the Society be expanded by establishing member societies in the major provincial cities. According to Öttevényi, agitation was to be started in already-existing societies. The member organizations in the provinces were to keep in touch with the Society in Budapest and with each other. Together, they were to bring strong pressure on the Assembly. This would-be Jacobin also recommended the holding of political banquents.

Although a number of journalists spoke in favor of Öttenvényi's proposals, László Madarász, perhaps wishing to guard his position of leadership or merely because he was more realistic, argued that the

Society lacked the means to accomplish all this. The Society did not have the money to start organizing the countryside as yet, but, he said, those who wanted to try should, by all means, go ahead.[34]

Two days later the Society held another meeting, prompted possibly by the Assembly's passage of the army organization bill. The pamphleteer Birányi spoke to the audience:

> "Let us not forget that modest associations often develop strength sufficient to overthrow state power. I do not wish to recommend to the Society that it take violent steps for the overthrow of the government, because that would be illegal, and illegal actions are sanctified only by the product of rapidly-moving events, by revolution. I only call the attention of the Society to the power which lies hidden in it and which it has to develop. . . . It is the duty of the Society to develop this power, especially at a time when the fatherland is in danger and the government has proved itself incapable of saving it and the Assembly is also proving itself to be incapable."[35]

Birányi then stressed that he did not mean to incite revolution, but it is difficult to interpret his words otherwise. Clearly, he was seeking action against the Government and the Assembly. Among others, he specifically recommended that the "forces of March" be brought together because "these promised to be strong elements in a truly patriotic transformation." He also wished to hold a public meeting to enlighten the people about the Society's patriotic intentions and to gain further strength from the audience.

During an extraordinary meeting on August 23, the Society set the date of September 8 for such a meeting which would be followed by a banquet to be attended by all members of the Society from Budapest and the countryside. The date was well-chosen for it was a market day and large numbers of people were expected to be in Budapest.

Meanwhile, at the Society's meetings denunciations of the Government became intensified. Vasvári believed that the Assembly had set itself against the nation by passing the army bill and felt that the Society should mobilize public opinion against the Assembly to prevent the implementation of the law.[36] Another radical intellectual denounced all those who did not believe Hungary capable of organizing her military forces independently as "internal enemies" and warned that they were more to be feared than external enemies.[37] The reference to internal enemies was not an isolated incident. Petőfi wrote that now was the time for the nation to rise and strike out at its enemies with the force of lightning:

"Where is the enemy, you ask? Don't ask.
He is everywhere you look.
And, the greatest and most dangerous is he
Who, as a brother, clings to our breasts.
The greatest enemy is among us,
Villainous traitorous brothers!
One of them destroys hundreds,
Like a drop of poison in a glass of wine.
The death sentence to them!
Even if the executioner must strike a
 hundred thousand blows,
Even if the blood which flows
Would flood through the windows
 of the houses from the streets."[38]

The metaphor of the last verse smacks of wild romanticism. Petőfi certainly did not want a blood bath to eliminate Hungary's internal enemies. But he was willing to get rid of the enemies, if necessary, through violent means.

In a personal letter to a friend written at this time, Petőfi says: "I believe that we are on the eve of a great revolution, and you know that I do not have false suspicions. Then our fist task will be to erect immense gallows and [hang] nine people on it."[39] Clearly, this was a reference to the nine Cabinet members.

And, again in a poem entitled "Revolution," Petőfi commented on the events. The times are bad and the days are black because the leaders have deserted their people. He called his song the forerunner of revolution.[40]

# CHAPTER XIV
# THE HUNGARIAN SEPTEMBER DAYS

## A. *The possibility of a second revolution**

Petőfi talked privately and publicly about a second revolution. The official newspaper of the Society for Equality gave every indication that the dissatisfaction with the Government had become stronger.[1] A conservative deputy wrote that the streets and public places in Budapest were filled with officers of the newly-formed national defense units speaking out angrily against the Palatine and reactionary ministers and swearing that they would rid the capital of them in a few days.[2]

The *March Fifteenth* gave similar indications of an impending confrontation with the Government. On September 1, in reply to an attack from the Government press, the paper described itself for the first time as the "journal of revolution and barricades."[3]

That there was great anticipation concerning the banquet, becomes even more obvious from contemporary private letters. A young man, probably a member of the Society, wrote on August 25 from Budapest to his friend in the provinces: "Come up for the banquet—it will be on September 8—[there will be] a big popular meeting and after that the banquet. If more of you come from Almás (the recipient's home town), it would not hurt. All of you should read *Democracy* and pay attention to the meetings of the Equality Club because it has a great future."[4]

While friends of the Society were predicting it would have a "great future," others were fearing it would mean serious trouble. The adjutant of Archduke Stephen, Count Albert Zichy, a major in the Imperial army, wrote to a fellow officer in Italy that things in Budapest could not continue much longer as they were, and that it was an open secret that the radicals would attempt to force the resignations of all the Ministers with the exceptions of Kossuth and Szemere, by the means of a banquet at which 15,000 peasants would take part.[5]

The fears of the aristocratic army officer in the Palatine's entourage were reiterated by a Transylvanian deputy, Károly Topler, after he attended a meeting of the Society. On September 4, in a letter[6] to a friend, Topler described Budapest as living through scenes resembling the first years of the French Revolution. He admitted that there was as yet no bloodshed, but that there were many who wanted to bring it about in order to assume power. He said that daily bad news from the Servian front and the preparations of Jellačić created great excitement in the capital. Madarász and his followers were taking advantage of the reverses and were blaming the Government for them, wrote Topler, in order to ". . .incite the people to the highest degree. Then they will hold their state-wide banquet which is planned for September 8. . . . On that occasion, it is their purpose to overthrow the Government through a magnificent popular demonstration. After seizing power, it is their plan to convert everyone to patriotism through Robespierrean terrorism."

In the rest of the letter, Topler described a meeting of the Society held on September 3,[7] at which there was open incitement to rebellion. Vasvári demanded that Hungary follow the example of France and save herself from foreign enemies and royalists through an enlightened dictatorship. "The Cabinet should be set aside and those who think themselves capable should take the Government into their own hands. They should guillotine the leaders to save the fatherland!" Topler commented on Vasvári's call by saying, "You cannot imagine my dear friend, how numerous are those who would find the roles of Robespierre, Danton, Hebert and others of their ilk, suitable for themselves. Everyone who made a speech and won applause thinks himself destined to make his name shine through the country by wielding the sword of terrorism and beheading a few thousand rebels." These accounts make it apparent the Society for Equality was contemplating decisive action in those early September days.

The question arises whether the radicals had a serious chance of success. Since the Society's membership was around one thousand[8], it was unlikely that they could take over a country of 15 million against the wishes of the population. But history provides many examples of small minorities near the center of power having a decisive influence on the outcome of events. This seems to be especially true if in crisis conditions those in power are unable to provide leadership. In Hungary during those days in late August and early September, such a situation was developing.

The Government attempted to deal with the Serbian uprising and the threatening dangers from Croatia by sending Batthyány and Deák to Vienna. Their mission was to persuade the King to sanction the army bill and to obtain assurances of support from the Court against Jellačić. Batthyány and Deák, as the King's Ministers, were following legal procedures. A great deal depended upon the outcome of their mission and it would have meant a great victory for Batthyány's policy if the Court agreed to a separate Hungarian army and made firm commitments against Jellačić. The immediate problems of the country might have been solved peacefully and the radicals of the Society for Equality would have been rebels without a cause.

If the Court did not approve the army bill, the Cabinet either had to resign or to implement the bill without royal approval. The latter course of action would have meant a departure from legal procedures, something that Batthyány was unlikely to do. Thus, in the event of a refusal, a Cabinet crisis could be expected and would have created an excellent opportunity for the radicals to attempt a seizure of power.

On September 2 nothing definite was known in Budapest about Batthyány's mission. Kossuth informed the House that Batthyány and Deák were holding crucial negotiations on that very day with the King, and asked for everyone's cooperation for the maintenance of peace and order.[9]

Kossuth's request is the probable cause for the Society's surprising decision to postpone its coming banquet. After all, the preparations had been made, the public expectations aroused, and Vasvári's demands to use the guillotine if necessary were formulated. At the September 3 meeting a journalist named Kocsis suggested that a proclamation be issued immediately. From the rather brief description given in the *Radical Democrat*, it was clear that the journalist had a call to arms in mind. "This proposal was met with many opposing views because circumstances have not matured enough to follow this course of action," the paper reported. *"What we have to do, we will do in due course. As long as it is possible, we should use light weapons. There will be a time for the heavy ones also.*"[10] (Italics mine.)

Following the report of the Society's meeting there was an article in which the readers were informed that because public attention was occupied with the problem of saving the country, and because many young men were absent from the capital, the Society had decided to postpone the banquet planned for September 8. No new date was set, but the possibility of a banquet was reserved for a later time.

In following Kossuth's pleas to suspend action, the radicals subordinated their interests as a political faction to national interests. It is also probable that they felt they did not have enough strength to act. The reference to the absence of young men from Budapest points to this.

Even assuming that the revolutionary intellectuals and their radical friends in the Assembly were just waiting for a more favorable opportunity to carry out a coup d'état, their behavior on September 3 indicates that they were capable of analyzing the political merits of such an action. By withholding their plans, they did not provide the Court with an excuse to break off the negotiations with Batthyány or to refuse his demands on the grounds that revolutionary disturbances were going on in Budapest.

B. *The King against the nation.*

But the Court apparently did not wait for an excuse to begin hostilities against Hungary. On August 31, the Austrian Cabinet issued a long memorandum which in substance denied Hungary's right to independence. The memorandum claimed that an independent, responsible Cabinet for Hungary, particularly with respect to the Ministries of War, Finance and Foreign Affairs, was incompatible with the unity of the Habsburg Empire. It denied the Monarch's right to sanction the April Laws, which had re-established the independence of Hungary; it flatly stated that a "Hungarian Kingdom separate from the Austrian Empire was a political impossibility;" and it demanded the re-establishment of "common state government."[11]

King Ferdinand sent this memorandum to the Palatine with a letter emphasizing the necessity of re-establishing the "unity of government" and expressing his approval of the memorandum. Ferdinand also ordered several Hungarian Cabinet members to Vienna for negotiations.[12]

The lack of good faith implicit in this letter is underscored by the fact that Batthyány and Deák were in Vienna when the memorandum was issued. In spite of their desire to normalize relations with the Court, they found themselves unable to make any progress. No one would enter into substantial negotiations with them despite their repeated requests to the Monarch and their attempted contacts with members of the dynasty and even with the Austrian War Minister, Count Latour.[13]

Since the Hungarian Government was willing at this point to agree to the separation of Croatia from Hungary,[14] it would have been easy for the Court to avert the impending war if it so desired. Instead, on September 4, Ferdinand sent a letter to Jellačić, reinstating him as viceroy of Croatia in recognition of his faithfulness to the dynasty and to the interests of the "Gesamtmonarchie."[15]

The memorandum and the reinstatement of Jellačić mark the point at which the Court openly began its attempts to revoke the concessions granted in April. The Court was now in a stronger position because by September 1848 the revolutionary tide had lost a great deal of momentum all over Europe. Field Marshal Radetzky had won a decisive victory at Custozza in Italy and had re-established Habsburg rule in Lombardy. It appeared that the Imperial army stood by the

Emperor victoriously and that the Emperor no longer felt obligated to fulfill his responsibilities as King of Hungary.

Reacting to the memorandum in the Assembly, Kossuth predicted that without a drastic improvement in the situation, the Government which had taken an oath to the King and the Constitution would not be able to save the country from the impending dangers. He added, "The nation will be forced to provide itself temporarily with such executive power which will not have to derive its means of procedure from the law, but from the need to protect the fatherland."[16]

Kossuth's willingness to depart from legality when there seemed to be no alternative to retain the accomplishments of the March Days brought him very close to the radicals of the Society for Equality. But Kossuth wished to try once more with the Court. He suggested that not ministers, but a delegation from the Assembly should go to Vienna to clarify matters.

Kossuth's suggestion was accepted by the Assembly. A delegation of 100 deputies and 40 members of the House of Lords, led by the Speaker of the House, Dénes Pázmándy, took the steamer to Vienna. Pázmándy, in a respectful but firm speech, reminded the Monarch that Hungary was not a province occupied by force of arms, but a free country whose constitutional independence His Majesty had sworn to uphold at his coronation. He pointed out that there was a rebellion in Hungary, the leaders of which openly declared that they rebelled in the name and in the interest of the King and the dynasty against the Hungarian Government. Pázmándy told Ferdinand that the nation wished the King would support the legislature with the weight of his dignity. He should order all his subjects in Hungary to obey the law and, by coming to Budapest, the King could help and lead the constitutional authorities to establish peace and order.[17]

The King answered that he was sorry he could not go to Budapest because of his ill health, but that he would examine the proposals of the delegation. He promised to uphold the integrity of Hungary and indicated that he would express his intentions through the Cabinet soon.

In deep silence the delegation left the place and took the steamer back to Budapest. According to the British Ambassador in Vienna, ". . .they left Vienna having hoisted the red flag and wearing red cockades and feathers in their hats."[18]

C. *Radicals in the political crisis caused by the counterrevolutionary attack.*

While the Hungarian Government and Assembly were making final attempts to come to terms with Ferdinand, the radical press cut short its criticism. On September 4 the *March Fifteenth* approved the Assembly's decision to send the delegation to Vienna, saying that the Cabinet had acted with spirit and the National Assembly had behaved with dignity.[19] The *Radical Democrat* was also pleased. A front-page editorial by József Madarász declared: "This is the way we will save our country." Stating that the radicals did not necessarily want to put new people in the government by force and if the government was willing ". . . to raise the standard of the holy principles of the revolution," he was willing to forget the past and to support the Cabinet in a new and decisive course of action.[20]

As József Madarász was a leading member of the Society for Equality and published this article in its official journal, we can assume that he expressed the prevailing opinion of the radicals when the delegation made its trip. This opinion seemed to be that of "wait and see," at least for the moment. While they were waiting, the radicals also were making preparations.

The Society for Equality did not hold its banquet, but it did call a huge meeting on the eighth of September, where it was decided to establish a permanent committee to keep watch on the political situation. Among the committee's members were such well-known figures as Petőfi, Vasvári, Jókai, Nyári, Perczel, the Madarász brothers, Táncsics, Pálffy, the actor Egressy, the leading statistician Fényes, and several lesser known but not less radical journalists. These men were divided into four groups, relieving each other every six hours. The Society announced the formation of its vigilante committee to the citizens by posters, and called upon them to pass on any information to the committee. In addition, it was decided to form a private "national defense" force of 1,000 men divided into 10 companies, under the command of Perczel. Among the "captains" of this force we find Petőfi, Vasvári and Csernátoni, the associate editor of the *March Fifteenth*.

The Society apparently had some sort of arsenal of its own, because it promised to provide arms to those not able to arm themselves. The volunteers, in turn, swore upon their honor as patriots to obey the orders of their superiors and to defend the constitution. Recruitment was to be handled by the vigilante committee. This force, however, was not planned as a permanent body. The Society would keep the 1,000 men under arms for only three days—until September 12.[21]

These plans were communicated to the public in the *Radical Democrat* and on posters. How much of the radicals' plans was withheld cannot be determined because there is no information on the details even in memoirs written several decades after the events.[22] Only a conservative political opponent, a deputy named Lajos Kovács, accused the party of the *March Fifteenth* and the Madarász brothers of preparing lists of names of those whom they were planning to "proscribe."[23]

Although the Society did not give specific reasons for the formation of a private army, the fact that it was to be maintained from September 10 to 12 provides certain clues. The parliamentary delegation was expected to return from Vienna during these three days. It was obvious that if it brought a refusal, the Cabinet would resign, with two possible consequences. First, a new cabinet might be formed, but if this proved impossible, a general crisis would result. In view of the hostile attitude of the Court, it was unlikely that the Court would designate a Prime Minister who could win the confidence of a majority in the Assembly. Therefore, a crisis could reasonably be expected, and then the time would come for the revolutionary, extra-legal executive power. From the tone of their newspapers, it seems likely that the radicals wanted to establish revolutionary executive power only if no other solution was found. Thus, they were in substantial agreement with Kossuth. Since Kossuth was the most popular political figure in the country and he was willing to depart from legal means barring any other solution, it is highly probable that the radicals wanted to have their private army in readiness to seize power with Kossuth.

As in March, the radicals again in September provided an alternative to legality. There are additional parallels between the two periods. Archduke Stephen again informed the Court about the dangerous situation and asked for discretionary power to dissolve the Assembly and to prevent "banquets, popular meetings and other such revolutionary demonstrations."[24] But while in March the Court had followed the Palatine's advice, in September it felt strong enough to carry out its own plans. Stephen was informed that discretionary power for him was superfluous.[25]

It is a supreme irony of history that Kossuth wanted to persuade this treacherous prince, whom he considered to be a Hungarian patriot, to accept the Crown of Hungary. The dramatic offer of the Crown to Archduke Stephen was made in a private conversation in the middle of the night while Batthyány, Deák and the Assembly's delegation were still in Vienna. Kossuth warned the Archduke that under the circumstances Ferdinand could not retain the Crown, and that it would be best for Hungary and for the Habsburg dynasty if Stephen became King. Stephen refused. The conversation between them remained secret and the political situation did not change.[26]

While the Palatine was contemplating counterrevolution and Kossuth was thinking of a palace revolt, Batthyány took steps to maintain the law. He arranged for several regiments to be sent to Budapest to reinforce the garrison.[27] The unexpected appearance of these troops in Budapest undoubtedly was a factor in neutralizing the Society for Equality.

In addition, the police chief, Pál Hajnik, dissolved the Society after the formation of the vigilante committee and the call for a private army were made public.[28] The dissolution was not taken seriously, however, and the Society continued to function, holding public meetings and demonstrations and issuing manifestoes. But the organization of the private army was prevented by the prohibition. The "dissolved" Society informed the public the day following the first call to arms that the organization of any "national defense" force had been forbidden until further notice by the Assembly.[29]

The situation developed in such a way that by the time the Assembly delegation returned, there was no need to carry out a second revolution. The Palatine attempted to take the reins of government into his own hands but gave the idea because the Assembly declared his move illegal. Batthyány recommended to the deputies that the nation's fate be entrusted to Kossuth, who had the confidence of the nation as well as that of the Assembly. At first, Kossuth seemed willing and promised to form a Cabinet in five minutes. But the next day, when it was revealed that the Palatine had asked Batthyány to form a new Cabinet, Kossuth gave his support to him and convinced the Assembly to do the same.[30]

Between September 12 and 25, Batthyány made repeated attempts to form a new cabinet. These efforts were unsuccessful because the Court would not confirm his appointments despite the fact that he included only moderates whose loyalty to the Crown was general knowledge. Kossuth's name was absent from any of the new ministerial combinations.

Kossuth in no way hindered Batthyány's efforts. For the most popular political figure in the country, a man obviously desiring power, he exercised remarkable self-restraint. The reason he stated to the Assembly:

> "He who wishes the country well has to follow a policy which will accomplish two ends. One is to see that intrigue and treason are eliminated or, without pretext, exposed as intrigue, treason, reaction and nothing else. We will achieve a great deal if we can do this. The other goal is to see that until the nation succeeds in the first, she should get prepared."[31]

Kossuth's appraisal was correct. In Hungary, where royalism was deeply ingrained in the public mind despite all the efforts of the radicals, it was necessary to make it absolutely clear that the nation was the victim of aggression. The counterrevolution provided the proof of his point. Jellačić attacked Hungary on September 11, crossing the Drava River, the frontier between Hungary and Croatia, with an army of 40,000 men. Jellačić issued a proclamation to the Hungarians promising them peace, order and freedom from the tyranny of the ministry in Budapest.[32]

When this proclamation was issued, there was no ministry in Budapest, only a designated Prime Minister. Kossuth, although officially only a deputy in the Assembly, became the greatest force in the resistance to Jellačić. On Kossuth's motion the House ordered the immediate organization of the armed force it had approved in August. All new military units were organized into national defense (*honvéd*) battalions under Hungarian colors and command. Officers and enlisted men of the Imperial army were authorized to join the newly-formed battalions at once.

This was the first step in the organization of a large Hungarian national army. The Hungarians responded enthusiastically to the call and it was a strong indication that Hungary would not give up her rights without a serious struggle.

The Assembly also passed two acts which benefitted both the peasants and the nobles, with the intent of bolstering their patriotism. The feudal dues on vineyards were abolished and compensation was promised to the nobility.[33] On Kossuth's recommendation, the second law assumed debts of the nobles who would have money owed to them for their losses suffered through the abolition of serfdom.[34] Under certain conditions, the state began to make advance payments.

The Assembly—again on Kossuth's suggestion—determined to make one last attempt to avert a break with Austria. Having failed with the dynasty, it now decided to send a delegation to the Austrian Parliament, to suggest solidarity between the peoples of Hungary and Austria and to declare Hungary's desire to work out all the difficulties. The Imperial Parliament did not even receive the delegation. Deák, who led the delegation, was politely informed that if he had something to say, it should be communicated in writing.[35]

This added insult to injury. As the British Ambassador in Vienna observed, the representatives of a sovereign nation were treated as petitioners.[36] The Hungarians chose to fight Jellačić. But, against the invading army of 40,000, there was a weak force of about 5,000, mostly untrained recruits and National Guards. Under the command of an Imperial general, by birth a Hungarian aristocrat, Count Ádám Teleki, this force retreated in the direction of the capital without offering any resistance. It became clear that Á. Teleki was not guided by military considerations alone, in his retreat. A dispatch of September 15 from Teleki's army informed the House that the general was not willing to fight against Jellačić, who had taken the same oath that he had.

Teleki not only declared his neutrality, but threatened to go over to Jellačić if supplies were not received from the Hungarians.[37] In this emergency, Batthyány rose to the occasion. He persuaded the Assembly to call upon the Palatine to take command of the country's forces as Captain General of Hungary. Archduke Stephen accepted and went to join the army. Since Jellačić was not willing to negotiate with Stephen and the Archduke had received orders from Ferdinand not to enter into armed conflict with the Croats, the Palatine resigned his office and left for Vienna on September 23.[38] Thus, the country was deserted by its highest public official and was left entirely to its own resources at a time when an invading army was making steady progress toward Budapest.[39]

The radicals, however, were not passive. Although their September plans had come to naught, they had helped to arouse the public. After the return of the Assembly delegation from Vienna, the news of the Cabinet's resignation drew thick crowds on the streets.[40] The Society for Equality organized a big public meeting for September 12 to give direction to popular sentiment. The location was the same as during the March Days, the square before the National Museum. The meeting ended by calling for Kossuth's appointment as Prime Minister and asking the Palatine to act vigorously in the interests of the country in cooperation with Kossuth.[41]

Kossuth's reply was that, even if he did not become Prime Minister, he would do all in his power to serve the country and he added that his strength was proportionate to the support he received from the enthusiasm of the nation.[42]

In the Assembly too, Kossuth repeatedly sided with the radicals. He warned the deputies not to be more fearful of the overzealous actions of the nation's friends than they were of the nation's enemies.[43] On the everpresent question of legality, Kossuth stated that he was very much for following legal forms, but only provided the King was equally bound by them. He said, further, that he did not know of a more dangerous version of tyranny than that which used legality as a pretext to destroy the law and constitution.[44]

A few days later, Kossuth arrived at the idea that the Assembly was supreme in the nation and that, aside from deposing the King, anything the law-making body decided was legal.[45] These statements gave Kossuth increased support from all Magyars. The next day the *March Fifteenth* stated: "Hungary can be saved only by concentrated dictatorial power and . . . this power must be given to Kossuth."[46] Similarly, József Madarász wrote in the *Radical Democrat* that he and other deputies in the Assembly wanted more action from the Government than Batthyány had been able to generate, and that they wanted to have a new government under the "presidency of Kossuth."[47]

The radicals in the Assembly also voiced loud support for Kossuth. When Batthyány announced he had been asked to form a new cabinet, he received cheers from the right. The deputies on the left, however, responded with shouts of "Long live Kossuth!"[48] On September 14, Batthyány was denounced by László Madarász and compared unfavorably with Kossuth. A little later, another deputy proposed a motion of no confidence in Batthyány and urged Kossuth should be entrusted with the government.[49]

The radicals also succeeded in mobilizing support for Kossuth among the people of Budapest, who once more became a very significant factor in national politics. The demonstrations began after the resignation of the Batthyány Cabinet and continued throughout the month of September. A conservative deputy, commenting on the composition of the crowds, wrote: "He, who looked at the rabble stationed around the Assembly building, could not see one single reputable burgher from Pest. They were people collected by Madarász and his comrades."[50]

Since those who are opposed to revolutions usually call demonstrators "rabble" one might have doubts about the first part of this statement. The second part seems to be supported by the fact that the Speaker of the House usually solved the problem of noise by calling upon Nyári and Madarász to quiet the crowd, which they did by speaking from the balcony of the Assembly building.

The crowds never entered the Assembly nor caused harm to the deputies, and as the Speaker could always keep the galleries quiet, there have never been charges that free decision-making was interfered with during September. But it must have given additional strength to the radicals in the Assembly to have their cheers for Kossuth echoed outside by the dense crowds.

Radical agitation was quite effective even amon the enlisted men of the Imperial Army. As the Assembly ordered the establishment of Hungarian battalions, Perczel and other radicals persuaded many Hungarian soldiers to join the newly-formed Hungarian battalions.

Since Hungarian uniforms were not available, these soldiers stripped the black and yellow ribbons from their uniforms to symbolize that they had ceased to be soldiers of the House of Austria.[51] The patriotism of some went to such a degree that they cut off the tails of their frock coats so that there would be no question of whose soldiers they were![52]

With no significant regular army to defend Budapest against Jellačić, several volunteer units were organized in the capital and named after Hunyadi, Zrinyi and other popular figures from Hungarian history. Perczel became the leader of one such volunteer unit and was soon to distinguish himself in action.

It also became imperative to mobilize the peasantry. Even Batthyány realized this and as Prime Minister he ordered general mobilization in the Transdanubian area.[53] Petőfi, Vasvári, József Madarász and other members of the Society for Equality all spent shorter or longer periods in the provinces, rousing the peasants to the danger and persuading them to take up arms against the enemy.[54]

Táncsics, who had faithfully represented the cause of the peasantry since March, now urged them to set aside old grievances and to join with their former masters in the defense of the country. He even wrote and printed a manifesto in his *Workers' Newspaper* calling on the peasants to take up arms, warning that the victory of Jellačić would mean the restoration of feudal burdens.[55]

On behalf of the Society for Equality, Petőfi wrote a similar proclamation. He warned the peasants that they would become beasts of burden again if they welcomed Jellačić. He told them they should stand up and fight in the life and death struggle as befitted a free people.[56]

These efforts were quite successful. After the initial shock, the peasants engaged in large-scale guerilla warfare against Jellačić's troops. They cut off his supply lines from Croatia by capturing his wagon trains and, at times, his mail also.[57] Thus, in addition to mobilizing popular support for Kossuth, the radicals also made an important contribution to the national effort against the foreign invasion.

D. *Establishment of the Committee of National Defense.*

In the middle of September, Kossuth moved in the Assembly to form a House Committee to gather military information which would be kept confidential. He believed that some House members should be informed of military matters so that recommendations could be made to the Assembly at large.

This proposal sounded somewhat unclear, particularly for the extremely articulate Kossuth. If confidential matters had to be discussed, the procedure of a closed session of the Assembly could be used. But, it appears, as early as September 15 Kossuth wished to have some control over the Prime Minister and, in this way, a share in power.

Batthyány replied to Kossuth that he would willingly give information either to the Assembly or to a committee at any time, but that as long as he held his office he wanted a free hand in regard to executive power. He added if the Assembly did not approve, he was ready to resign immediately.

Kossuth explained that he merely wanted the committee to gather information, not to exercise authority, and repeated his request that the committee be formed.[58] According to József Madarász, after Kossuth made his proposal, 10 or 12 radical deputies sat down to determine whom they would support for membership on the committee. They quickly agreed on Kossuth, László Madarász, Nyári and a Transylvanian named Pálffy. József Madarász decided upon the two remaining places to go to Patay and Zsemberey.

A few hundred ballots were prepared with the names of the radical candidates. What happened is worth quoting from Madarász's memoirs:

> "On the 16th, during the afternoon session, the printed ballots were put on my desk and everything proceeded as I had predicted. . . .The former opposition [i.e., radicals] used the ballots spread in front of me. Since it was impossible for the members of the former government party not to notice this, they too came over to us in great numbers and, finding our candidates acceptable, voted for them. The audience in the galleries noisily cheered the members of the opposition as they entered the hall. This may have contributed to the victory of the minority ballot. The chief reason for our victory, however, was that the country experienced dangerous moments when the House did not know whether there would be a cabinet or if it would collapse. On such an occasion the greater majority yields to the vigorous minority."[59]

After the election of the radical slate was made public, Kossuth pushed to change the nature of the committee. He pointed out to the Assembly that it was impossible for one man to carry the full responsibility of the government and to handle all aspects of national defense. László Madarász added that the Prime Minister had too much to do, therefore, the House should create an executive power.[60]

Deák opposed Kossuth and Madarász and again Batthyány declared that he did not need assistance. Also, he again threatened to resign if any other executive power were established.[61] Thus, the moderates retained control and a new, massive act of hostility from the Court was needed to press the Assembly into a break with Vienna.

In the meantime, Jellačić's troops had occupied Székesfehérvár, a city about 40 miles from the capital. Budapest resembled an armed camp. The inhabitants were building fortifications and making other defensive preparations. Volunteers were pouring into the city, many peasants armed only with scythes. Fifteen hundred Viennese arrived to fight for Hungary's freedom, and about 100 Frenchmen of Budapest also marched off to fight Jellačić singing the Marseillaise.[62]

Kossuth left the capital for the central part of Hungary to recruit volunteers. At his request, a small band of armed youth, with Jókai among them, accompanied him. His success as an orator was never greater. After his speeches thousands flocked to join the National Guard. Toward the end of his career, Jókai wrote that he had never experienced anything as thrilling: "I saw this giant spirit who woke the people up from their deathly dream. I listened to his words, which created heroes out of peaceful citizens; armed ranks grew from the soil; in a few days a hundred thousand men stood armed under the flag, ready to die in the defense of the country."[63]

The novelist's romantic description was essentially accurate. Three days later, Kossuth returned to the capital and reported to the Assembly that about 12,000 men were on their way to the front.[64]

The threatening danger bolstered the national unity of the Magyars. There were only six members of the Assembly, representing Transylvanian Germans, who did not identify with the national cause. Using the excuse that the Assembly had ordered the establishment of a national army without royal sanction, they resigned their Assembly seats. Kossuth accused them of treason and insisted that they should keep thier seats until new deputies could be elected to replace them.[65]

The *March Fifteenth* reacted even more violently. Pálffy used a wildly romantic metaphor and suggested that gallows be set up on the Square of Liberty and a guillotine elsewhere and they be used to eradicate treason. He warned that an association had been formed recently to find traitors and hang them.[66] The reign of terror Pálffy recommended could not be introduced because there did not seem to be any traitors. Still, it is likely that such articles served to intimidate foes of the revolution enough to keep them quiet.

In any case, the Government was soon attaacked by the Court. On September 25, Ferdinand issued a manifesto to the peoples of Hungary informing them that he had appointed Lieutenant Field Marshal Francis Lamberg as commander-in-chief of the armed forces in Hungary. In somewhat ambiguous language, the manifesto stated that

Lamberg's mission was to stop bloodshed and to re-establish law and order, as well as harmony with the other parts of the Empire.[67]

Since the King had accused the Hungarian Government and the Assembly of numerous unlawful acts in another manifesto issued a few days before, the appointment of Lamberg appeared to be an attempt to disarm Hungary and the first step toward dissolving the Assembly.[68]

While Batthyány was in the field with the army opposing Jellačić, the manifesto appointing Lamberg arrived in Budapest on September 27, together with the news that Batthyány's proposed cabinet had been rejected by the Court. Baron Vay, a conservative politician, was asked to form a new cabinet. Thirty-one radical deputies asked for an extraordinary session of the Assembly, which was called for 11:00 p.m.

László Madarász brought Kossuth back from his recruiting trip at once and was the first speaker at this late night meeting. Madarász angrily declared Ferdinand's latest manifesto illegal, null and void, and urged the House to forbid Lamberg from assuming command over Hungary's troops. Kossuth denounced the manifesto and cited as evidence of its illegality Article III, Section 3 of the April Laws which stated: "Any decrees, orders, decisions or appointments of His Majesty are valid only if they are countersigned by one of the resident ministers in Budapest."[69]

Since Lamberg's appointment had not been countersigned, Kossuth's accusation was correct. The Assembly adopted his resolution, which quoted Article III, declaring Lamberg's appointment illegal, null and void, and forbidding Lamberg to occupy his position "in the name of the law." It also forbade anyone to follow Lamberg's orders. The resolution concluded with the promise that the representatives of the nation were determined to defend the constitution.[70]

The next morning Lamberg arrived at the Buda garrison. There is no evidence that he knew of the resolution passed in the late evening and it is unlikely that he did. Around 2:00 p.m. the news spread that Lamberg was coming to Pest. An excited crowd quickly gathered, which, according to the *March Fifteenth*, "seemed, for the most part, to be made up of the poorest class in the city." Some, however, were peasants armed with scythes on their way to the front. They stopped Lamberg on the bridge connecting Buda to Pest and brutally murdered him.[71]

There were no radical intellectuals or any known figures from the Left present. Afterwards, Pálffy wrote in the *March Fifteenth* that he did not know Lamberg's background but considered it possible that the unfortunate man was unaware of the nature of his mission and considered himself merely one commander replacing another. "This much is true: since the Austrian dynasty has been reigning the

Hungarian people have never committed such a deed. But now we must be consistent. If force is used against us, we must stand behind the barricades so none can say that these people who moved against one defenseless person in a mass behave in a cowardly fashion when attacked."[72]

On a motion by Kossuth, the Assembly passed a resolution condemning the assassination and ordering the city authorities to investigate and punish those responsible.[73] The radical Irinyi opposed Kossuth's motion. He claimed that Lamberg deserved to die except that first he should have been tried and sentenced. He considered it only a "mistake of form" and did not wish to give any instructions to the city authorities.[74]

In a poem written two months later, while the war with Austria was in full sway, Petőfi compared the incident with the murder of Count Latour in Vienna. These deaths meant to him that the people had begun to assume power, something he wanted wholeheartedly. He urged the peoples of the world to settle accounts with their oppressors for all time by hanging the kings.[75]

Even if the Assembly disapproved of Lamberg's murder, the deputies were ready to face the consequences of the action. Immediately after Kossuth's resolution was passed, the House instructed the Committee of National Defense consisting of six members "to assume the burden of responsibility until the return of the Prime Minister and to take charge of the defense of the country as well as the maintenance of peace and order." Although only three members of the Committee were present in Budapest, the Assembly granted them the authority to make valid decisions.[76]

A provisional government was now established. Executive power was retained by Kossuth and the other Committee members as Batthyány was no longer Prime Minister. Thus, an outburst of public anger and the Court's action gave Kossuth and László Madarász what they had not been able to get earlier from the Assembly.

The radicals came to power with the Committee of National Defense. Four of the six members belonged to the radical faction of the Assembly and all six were nominees of the radical minority. With Jellačić just a few miles from Budapest and violence within the city itself, the Assembly gave power to the faction which was ready to take it and showed promise of using it vigorously. This was a tremendous victory of the radicals, even if it did not prove to be a lasting one.

In analyzing the events which followed, a comparison with the French Revolution is tempting. Shortly after the Committee acquired power, the Hungarian army scored several victories over Jellačić. The main thrust of his army, under his personal command, was stopped at Pákozd, southwest of Budapest. Jellačić, who had promised to "liberate" Hungary from the tyranny of the ministry in Budapest after fighting one battle, retreated to Austria a few days later.

Jellačić's second major army corps, which he had left behind, was surrounded by large units of vollunteer National Guards (mainly peasants) under the command of Perczel, now a colonel. Perczel was ably supported by a former member of the Hungarian Royal Bodyguard, Arthur Görgey, who was destined to become the most famous as well as the most controversial soldier of the revolutionary war. General Roth, commander of Jellačić's second army corps, laid down his arms on October 7 before Perczel and Görgey. Two generals, three staff officers, about 50 officers, 7,500 non-commissioned officers and enlisted men and 12 cannons were captured.[77]

Thus, the invading troops left or were captured. The immediate danger was averted. As in France in the 1790's when power was given to the radicals, victory followed. But, although this was the case, it would be an exaggeration to attribute this success solely to radical leadership. It seems likely that victory was accomplished as a result of an effort to which Batthyány's attempts to preserve leagality and to organize Hungary's defenses also greatly contributed. In their efforts to avoid a fight with the Court and with Jellačić, the moderates, Batthyány and Deák, had placed the Court unimistakably in the wrong in the eyes of the Hungarians. The importance of this cannot be overestimated in a country where royalism was very deeply rooted. The Hungarians had a belief in the righteousness of the national cause which was shared alike by the land-owning gentry and the poorest peasants. This belief, although an intangible, counted for as much in this initial fighting as in the war that followed.

After Jellačić's defeat at Pákozd, new members were added to the Committee to emphasize that it represented both national and radical interests. First, four members of the Upper House volunteered and later two former Cabinet members, Szemere and Mészáros, joined the Committee. Characteristically, the Speaker of the Assembly recommended that they be placed on the Committee by referring to a widespread suspicion that the Committee was an "emanation of the minority." He suggested that such accusations could be answered best by the addition of four peers to the Committee.[78] So, in a time of extreme national danger, the Assembly gave power to the radicals, but once the crisis was over, it took back—or more precisely, forced the radicals to share it with the moderates.

The reduction in the proportionate strength of the radicals on the Committee of National Defense reflected the necessity of involving all sectors of the nation in the common effort. József Madarász, who was responsible for the original membership, accepted the new members with the comment that anyone who wanted to take part in saving the country should be welcomed.[79]

Even if the firm stand against Jellačić was due to the united national effort and the radicals had to share power with others, in setting up the revolutionary executive power the country followed policy that the radicals, and the radicals alone, had advocated from the beginning. The radical demand for a national Hungarian army became a reality by October. There is poetic justice in the fact that the deputy who demanded the national army the most loudly, Perczel, won the first victory with national troops. And, while the radicals remained in Hungary and fought, Batthyány, who with the best of intentions wanted peace, was in Vienna as a private citizen trying hopelessly to come to terms with the Court.

The Court, having received the news of Count Lamberg's murder but apparently not informed about the defeat and retreat of Jellačić, took a drastic step. On October 3, Ferdinand signed a decree dissolving the Assembly and making Jellacic commander in chief of all armed forces in Hungary. Jellačić was also give plenipotentiary powers as temporary viceroy.[80]

This decree clarified Austria's position toward Hungary. It placed the monarch at the head of the counterrevolution as represented by the military. From the viewpoint of the Hungarian Assembly and public opinion, the King sided with a traitor who was staging armed rebellion against the state. Hungarian national pride could not have been more insulted by the appointment of a Croat to pacify Hungary. To make matters worse, the decree was illegal. According to the consitution, the Assembly and making Jellačić commander-in-chief of all armed forces in Hungary. Jellačić was also given plenipotentiary powers as temporary viceroy.[80]

The dissolution of the Assembly and Jellačić's appointment were unfortunate measures on the part of the Court because they clearly could not serve their intended purpose. To appoint a general as commander-in-chief who, at that very moment, was trying to leave the country as fast as he could, made the Court look ridiculous. The Assembly's reaction to the decree was restrained. It declared on October 7 in a resolution that the decree could not possibly be from the King, but probably originated with those taking advantage of Ferdinand's ill health. If the decree was authentic, however, the resolution declared it to be null and void.[81]

The Assembly's real answer came the next day, when it placed the government of the country permanently in the hands of the Committee of National Defense. All powers were granted to the Committee which the Cabinet had previously held. "Citizen and Member of the Assembly, Kossuth" was named President of the new government, and he was charged with the responsibility of "fixing the tasks of the other members of the Committee."[82]

Thus, an extremely complex situation became greatly simplified. The King had set aside the constitution and attempted to govern against the wishes of his subjects by decree. The Assembly replied by defying royal authority and establishing a revolutionary national government. Since the radicals worked for the establishment of this government more assiduously than any other group, they were able to secure a share in the power. The break with the Court was complete. From that time on, only force of arms could decide between King and country.

## CHAPTER XV
## THE RADICALS AFTER THE SEPTEMBER DAYS

With the establishment of the Committee of National Defense and the beginning of the war, the significance of the radicals' activities began to decrease. The history of the war during the end of 1848 and in 1849 indicates that the radical faction did not substantially influence the outcome of events. Never again was there a possibility of their coming to power or even greatly influencing the political situation.

This reduced role of the radicals was due to a number of factors. The key to the remainder of the revolutionary period was provided when the Assembly made the Committee of National Defense the government of the country and called upon Kossuth "to fix the responsibilities of the other members of the Committee." Although Kossuth was not explicitly given dictatorial powers, even the text of the resolution made it clear that he was the unquestioned leader of the Hungarian nation until the end of the revolution. Kossuth enjoyed the full confidence of the Assembly and the nation because with immense energy and ability he organized the army and finances and took numerous recruiting trips to inspire unprecedented popular enthusiasm for the national cause.

The radicals had little reason to challenge Kossuth. There was complete accord between the radicals and Kossuth that the foremost task was to defend the nation against the King's troops and to bring the war to a victory. Without that victory, the radicals' plans to develop Hungary from a liberal into a democratic state could never materialize. Thus, with the start of the war, the radical cause merged with the national cause, and the radicals became the champions of the national cause above all.

After power was given to the Committee of National Defense, the radicals seized upon the opportunity to attempt to bring about the formal establishment of a republic. The *March Fifteenth* urged this action many times.[1] A law professor, Károly Kornis, wrote two pamphlets entitled "Manifesto to the People about the System of Government," recommending a republic over a monarchy.[2] A radical journalist and pamphleteer, Ákos Birányi, published a few issues of a propaganda sheet with the name *Republican Newspaper*.

The arguments for a republic stressed that it was the only rational form of government consonant with the principle of popular sovereignty. They rejected both absolute and constitutional monarchies, pointing out that a monarchy was expensive, superfluous and contrary to the interests of the people and that an elected president was more suitable than a hereditary ruler. The example of the United States was used repeatedly. Kornis wrote, "Look at America! There the republic, the government by the people, is 60 years old and this 60-year-old government by the people shows greater success than the kings of Europe can show from the beginning of the world."[3]

Birányi also published a *Republican Catechism* using the question and answer format, arguing that human happiness depended upon the belief that the republic was the "most perfect of all human conditions."[4] The most perfect republic, according to Birányi, would guarantee not only equality of rights, but also equality of means. Obviously very much under the influence of Louis Blanc, Birányi wrote that the "organization of labor" and "public workshops" would eliminate exploitation and bring a morally superior new age for mankind which he called communism.[5]

These views, though interesting in themselves, did not make a great impact and were ignored by the political leadership. A republic was not proclaimed. The public was preoccupied with the war. Many radical intellectuals believed the time for argument was over and words had to be followed by deeds. Petőfi, Vasvári, Egressy, Degré and Birányi, along with many more, joined the army. From radical agitators, they became army officers, away from Budapest, without any chance to exercise influence there. For Petőfi and Vasvári among others, it was a moral imperative to live their lives in harmony with their ideals and to fight on the battlefield for the freedom of Hungary.

The radical deputies did not remain inactive either. Perczel, a man of action rather than a parliamentarian, became a general and commanded a division. Irinyi and József Madarász were occasionally out of the capital on Assembly missions. The radical László Teleki, became Hungarian diplomatic representative in Paris where he tried unsuccessfully to secure diplomatic recognition for Hungary. He was absent throughout the whole revolution. Nyári and László Madarász assisted Kossuth with the organization of the war effort. The other two radical members of the Committee, Patay and Zsemberey, played an undistinguished role in political affairs.

Publication of the radical newspapers stopped. The *Radical Democrat* and *Workers' Newspaper* both came to an end in 1848. Only the *March Fifteenth* continued publication into 1849, but lost a great deal of its original fervor.

After the initial victory over Jellačić, the war brought serious reverses to the Hungarians. The Hungarian army stopped at the Austrian frontier, not wishing to pursue Jellačić on Austrian soil. After much delay, the Hungarians attempted to relieve the besieged Vienna revolutionaries. The Hungarian army was defeated at Schwechat, at the outskirts of Vienna, on October 30, 1848.

By December the new Austrian commander, Prince Windischgrätz, started a massive invasion of Hungary from the west. Other Austrian army troops were in northern Hungary, in Transylvania and in the south. The new, poorly-equipped Hungarian army had to fight on several fronts simultaneously. Windischgrätz defeated the Hungarians, and his troops entered Budapest on January 5, 1849.

The Austrian commander was certain that he had defeated the revolution and his campaign would soon be over, but Kossuth and his commanders proved him wrong. The Government and Assembly moved to Debrecen, a major city northeast of Budapest, and continued to organize resistance from there. The available Hungarian forces were concentrated in central Hungary, and in the spring, a major offensive under the command of Arthur Görgey drove the Austrians out of the country. Meanwhile, a Polish general in Hungarian seravice, Joseph Bem, cleared Transylvania of the enemy. By May 1848 it appeared that Hungary would become master of her destiny.

Because of the war the relationship with Austria and the dynasty remained unsolved for months. The Court had removed the mentally-retarded Ferdinand on December 2, 1848 and placed an 18-year-old prince, Francis Joseph, on the throne. The Assembly declared that the family arrangement was invalid until the Hungarian nation consented. No one could occupy Hungary's throne without swearing to respect the constitution and the laws of the country and being crowned with the Crown of St. Stephen.[6] Although the Assembly did not recognize Francis Joseph, the way was left open for "mutual agreement" between the new ruler and Hungary.

Under the influence of the winter victories of Windischgrätz, Francis Joseph issued a constitution on March 4, 1849. The document treated the Habsburg Empire as a unified centralized state, completely abolishing not only Hungary's independence but also dividing her territory into provinces to be governed directly from Vienna.[7]
Vienna.[7]

On Kossuth's recommendation, the Assembly gave a dramatic reply. Meeting in the large Calvinist church in Debrecen on April 14, 1849, the

Hungarian representatives declared the House of Habsburg-Lorraine dethroned, and communicated to the world that Hungary had re-entered the community of nations as a fully independent state, one and indivisible. It was also declared that, until the legislature determined the form of government, Hungary should be governed by "Governor-President" Lajos Kossuth and his appointed ministers.[8]

The dethronement of the ruling house was an act of great consequence. The decision of the Assembly was made not under the influence of the radical faction but under Kossuth's leadership.[9]

Some of the radicals even changed their political attachments while in Debrecen. Nyári joined the Peace Party which, before the Declaration of Independence, urged coming to terms with the Court. Nyári proposed to the Assembly that the nation should be ready at any time to conclude peace with the dynasty on the basis of the April Laws.[10] One of the heroes of the March Days, Jókai, now a journalist in Debrecen, joined Nyári and also became an advocate of peace.[11] Only a handful of deputies around the Madarász brothers remained radicals and continued to recommend a republic. About the Society for Equality, Táncsics had only this to say in his memoirs: "Although the Society for Equality still existed in Debrecen it seldom met and then finally dissolved itself."[12]

The influence of the radicals waned almost completely after László Madarász was accused of financial dishonesty and forced to resign both from the Committee and the Assembly.

The dethronement made reconciliation with the dynasty impossible, and Görgey's victories in the spring of 1849 gave weight to the Assembly's decision. But there was not time to consolidate internal conditions after the victories.

Russia, with England's approval, intervened in the war and Czar Nicholas sent a huge military force to aid his fellow monarch in Vienna. What the Austrian army had not been able to do alone, became possible with the Czar's aid. By June 1849, the combined Austro-Russian armies numbered 370,000 men equipped with 1,200 cannons. Against them Hungary put 152,000 men and 450 cannons in the field.[13]

The result of the unequal struggle was a foregone conclusion. By mid-August the War of Independence in Hungary came to an end with the defeat of the Hungarians. Kossuth went into exile and the remaining leaders faced the Austrian execution squads. Imperial absolutism was not maintained in Hungary for long, however. Less than two decades after the defeat, Francis Joseph was forced to re-establish a parliamentary constitutional state in Hungary. Some of the new liberties the nation had gained with the help of the radicals in the spring of 1848 were reinstated and formed the basis of the future development of Hungary.

## APPENDIX I
## DRAMATIS PERSONAE

ARANY, János (1817-1882). Poet, Petőfi's friend. Ran unsuccessfully for the Assembly in 1848; later enlisted in the National Guard. Considered to be the greatest Hungarian poet of the second half of the nineteenth century.

BATTHYÁNY, Count Lajos (1806-1849). Great estate owner, leader of the liberal opposition in Upper House before 1848. Prime Minister of the first responsible Hungarian cabinet (April 17-September 10, 1848). Made repeated attempts to come to terms with the Habsburgs in Sept. 1848. Arrested by the Austrians on Jan. 8, 1849 and excuted for high treason on Oct. 6, 1849. Considered a martyr for Hungary's freedom.

BIRÁNYI, Ákos (1816-1855). Journalist and pamphleteer; a member of the radical intelligentsia and eyewitness to the revolution in Budapest. Became an officer in the Hungarian revolutionary army.

BULYOVSZKY, Gyula (1827-1883). Journalist and lawyer, one of the organizers of the March 15 demonstration and member of the Committee of Public Safety in Budapest. In May 1848 he became an official in the Ministry of Interior. After 1848 dedicated himself entirely to jounalism and literature.

DEÁK, Ferenc (1803-1876). Gentry estate owner and an important leader of the liberal opposition in the Lower House before 1848. Became Minister of Justice in 1848. Remained liberal and moderate during the revolution but did not hold office after December 1848. The uncontested leader of Hungarian national opposition to Habsburg absolutism after 1849, he formulated the Compromise of 1867.

DEGRÉ, Alajos (1820-1896). Gentry writer and journalist. Petőfi's friend and a participant in the March 15 demonstration. Member of the Committee of Public Safety; later a cavalry captain in the Hungarian revolutionary army. Dedicated himself primarily to literature after 1849.

EGRESSY, Gábor (1806-1866). Radical actor and Petőfi's close friend. Member of the Committee of Public Safety. Official of the revolutionary government. Left Hungary in 1849 and was sentenced to death *in absentia* by the Austrians. Received amnesty and returned to Hungary in 1850's; dedicated himself entirely to the theatre thereafter.

ESTERHÁZY, Prince Pál (1786-1866). One of Europe's wealthiest aristocrats. Imperial ambassador to England. "Minister Near the Person of the King" in the first responsible cabinet in 1848. Resigned September 9, 1848 and retired from active politics.

IRÁNYI, Dániel (1822-1892). Lawyer and journalist, radical intellectual, member of the Committee of Public Safety in March. Radical deputy in the first representative Assembly and important "representative on mission" in 1848-49. Left Hungary in 1849 and was sentenced to death *in absentia* by the Austrians. Author (*see* Bibliography page 158). After 1867 returned to Hungary and became a member of Parliament. Was one of the leaders of the opposition to the 1867 Compromise.

IRINYI, József (1822-1859). Francophile radical lawyer, author and journalist. Drafted the Twelve Points during March 1848. Member of the Committee of Public Safety and later of the Assembly. Was sentenced to death but received amnesty. Dedicated himself to literature after 1850. Translated Stowe's *Uncle Tom's Cabin* into Hungarian.

JELLAČIĆ, Baron Joseph (1801-1859). Imperial army officer. Named viceroy of Croatia on March 23, 1848. Exploiting Croatian nationalism and with help from Vienna started war against revolutionary Hungary in September. One of the leaders of the Imperial army during the war against Hungary.

JÓKAI, Mór (1825-1904). Most popular Hungarian novelist. Romantic. In 1848 member of the radical intellignetsia and an organizer of the March 15 demonstration. Member of the Committee of Public Safety. Journalist during the revolution and a Peace Party member. After 1867 member of Parliament and a supporter of the Compromise.

KÁLLAY, Ödön (1815-1879). Gentry estate owner and county official. In 1848 a radical deputy and important member of the radical Assembly group. On his initiative the bill to emancipate the Jews was passed in the Assembly. Was sentenced to death after 1848 but received amnesty. A deputy again after 1867, he oposed the Compromise.

KECSKÉS, Ede (?-?) Radical lawyer. Agitated among the working class in Budapest the summer of 1848. Member of the Society for Equality.

KLAUZÁL, Gábor (1804-1866). Gentry estate owner and leader of the liberal opposition at the Diets. Joined the demonstration on March 15. Member of the Committee of Public Safety. Moderate. Minister of Agriculture, Industry and Commerce in the first responsible cabinet. Retired from politics at the end of 1848.

KOSSUTH, Lajos (1802-1894). Hungary's greatest national hero. Lawyer and journalist from the gentry. Entered politics in the 1830's in opposition to the government. Imprisoned between 1837-40 because of his political views. Editor of the largest Hungarian newspaper in the early 1840's. Advocated intransigent opposition to Vienna. Became the most influential member of the liberal opposition in the late 1840's. Elected deputy to the Lower House in 1847 from Pest county where he led the opposition until March 1848. Instrumental in enacting the April Laws which abolished feudalism and Hungary's dependence on Austria. Minister of Finance in the Batthyány cabinet and the speaker for the cabinet in the Assembly. Closer to the radicals than any other cabinet member. With their support he established a revolutionary government in September 1848. Organized and led Hungary's struggle for freedom in 1848-49. On his proposal, the Habsburgs were dethroned by the Assembly on April 14, 1849. "Governing-President" of Hungary from April 14-August 11, 1849. Exile in Turkey, England, U.S.A. and Italy thereafter. Received great sympathy in the West and remained in opposition to the Compromise. Died in exile.

LAMBERG, Count Ferenc (1791-1848). Lt. Fieldmarshal in the Imperial army. Ferdinand illegally appointed him Commander-in-Chief of all armed forces in Hungary. Murdered by a mob in Budapest Sept. 28, 1848.

LEDERER, Baron Ignác (1769-1849). Commander of the Buda garrison at outbreak of revolution. Antagonized the students and radical intellectuals. Hostile demonstration against him in May led to bloodshed. As a result, he was relieved of his command, transferred to Vienna and promoted to Fieldmarshal by the King.

MADARÁSZ, József (1814-1915). Gentry estate owner, lawyer, leader of the radical deputies in the Assembly. Co-editor of the *Radical Democrat* and founder of the Society for Equality. Imprisoned from 1849-1856. Became a deputy after 1867 and opposed the Compromise.

MADARÁSZ, László (1811-1909). Brother of József Madarász, also a lawyer. Leading radical deputy in the Assembly. Co-editor of the *Radical Democrat* and a founder of the Society for Equality. Member of Kossuth's revolutionary governmnet after Sept. 1848; generally was referred to as "police Minister." Accused of financial dishonesty by opponents in the Peace Party and forced out of politics. Left Hungary after 1848 and was sentenced to death *in absentia* by the Austrians. Became a farmer in Iowa where he lived until his death.

MÉSZÁROS, Lázár (1796-1858). Colonel of cavalry regiment in Italy before 1848. Corresponding Member of the Hungarian Academy of Sciences. War Minister in the Batthyány cabinet. Moderate. After September 1848 continued in his office and became a member of Kossuth's revolutionary government. Left Hungary after 1849 and was sentenced to death *in absentia* by the Austrians.

NYÁRI, Pál (1806-1871). Member of liberal opposition before 1848 and important official of Pest county. Joined the March 15 demonstration. Member of the Committee of Public Safety and later active radical deputy in the Assembly. Member of Kossuth's revolutionary government after September but later tended toward Peace Party. After 1849 sentenced to death by the Austrians but his sentence was changed to imprisonment where he spent seven years.

PATAY, József (1804-?). Gentry estate owner. Member of Committee of Public Safety. Radical deputy and member of Kossuth's revolutionary government but did not play leading role. Resigned due to ill health.

PÁLFFY, Albert (1820-1897). Came from well-to-do gentry. Studied for priesthood but left theological studies before ordination. Author of several novels and a journalist in Budapest. Petőfi's close friend and member of the radical intelligentsia. Founder and editor of the most important radical newspaper, the *March Fifteenth.* Member of the Society for Equality. After 1849 was in hiding for four years in a small Hungarian village. Interned in Budweis (Bohemia) between 1855-7 by the Austrians. Later dedicated himself to literature.

PÁLFFY, János (1814-1857). Belonged to liberal opposition before 1848 in Transylvania. Deputy in Assembly and member of Kossuth's revolutionary government after September. Resigned in January 1849 and sided with the Peace Party.

PÁZMÁNDY, Dénes (1816-1856). Gentry estate owner. Member of the liberal opposition before 1848. Speaker of the first representative assembly. In January 1849 resigned his mandate and went over to the Imperial side.

PERCZEL, Mór (1811-1899). Rich gentry estate owner with radical views even before 1848. Active participant in the March 15 demonstration. Member of the Committee of Public Safety. Resigned his high government office in protest against the moderate Batthyány Government. On the extreme left in the assembly. Was a general in the Hungarian revolutionary army. Exile, death sentence *in absentia* after 1849. Returned to Hungary after 1867 and became a deputy again on the left.

PETŐFI, Sándor (1823-1849). One of the greatest Hungarian poets. His father was a well-to-do butcher with a patent of nobility. Left private school when family lost its wealth and decided to be an actor. Traveled all over Hungary and at times lived in great poverty while writing some of the best of Hungarian poetry. From 1844 he lived in Budapest and was assistant editor of a literary magazine. A central figure of the young radical literati in Budapest, an organizer of the March 15 demonstration. Member of the Committee of Public Safety. Active extreme left agitator in the spring and summer of 1848. Failed in elections to assembly. Member of the Society for Equality. From Oct. 15 a captain and later a major in the Hungarian army. A republican, he strongly resisted any attempts to destroy the accomplishments of the revolution. Killed in battle on July 31, 1849, fighting the Russians.

PULSZKY, Ferenc (1814-1897). Liberal gentry politican before 1848. Archeologist and literary critic. Undersecretary in Batthyány Cabinet, he worked for the maintenance of peace and order during the March Days in Budapest. Supported Kossuth during the revolution and became Hungarian diplomatic representative in London in 1849. In exile from 1849-67. Later a deputy supporting the Compromise and director of the Hungarian National Museum. Author (*see* Bibliograhpy page 156.)

ROTTENBILLER, Lipót (1806-1870). Vice-burgomaster of Pest in March 1848. The Committee of Public Safety was established on his suggestion. Moderate. Mayor of Budapest during the summer of 1848.

SZEMERE, Bertalan (1812-1869). Gentry estate owner and a leader of liberal opposition at the Diet before 1848. Minister of the Interior in the Batthyány Cabinet. Member of Kossuth's revolutionary government after September and Prime Minister before the end of the revolution. Sentence to death *in absentia* by the Austrians. In exile 1849-65.

SZÉCHENYI, Count István (1791-1860). Great estate owner and initiator of reforms. Founder of the Hungarian Academy of Sciences and organizer of numerous projects of public improvement before 1848. According to Kossuth, the "greatest Hungarian." Minister of Public Works and Transportation in the Batthyány Cabinet. Saw the defeat of the revolution and suffered a nervous collapse on Sept. 5, 1848. Spent the last 12 years of his life in a mental institution.

TÁNCSICS, Mihály (1799-1884). Came from a family of serfs. Became a journeyman and later through self-education an assistant village teacher. Traveled on foot all over Europe.

Wrote many pamphlets and books attacking the feudal system in Hungary. Imprisoned at Buda between March 1847 and March 1848 for inciting against the established order. Liberated by the revolution on March 15. Editor of the *Workers' Newspaper* and radical deputy in the assembly. Member of the Society for Equality and on the extreme left in 1848-9. Hanged in effigy by the Austrians after 1849. Was in hiding in Hungary for eight years and later in prison for six years. Deputy after 1867 opposed to the Compromise. Champion of the industrial working class. Died in great poverty.

TELEKI, Count László (1811-1861). Great estate owner and leader of the liberal opposition before 1848. Also playwright and honorary member of the Hungarian Academy of Sciences. Radical deputy in 1848 belonging to the extreme left. Hungarian diplomatic representative in Paris after September 1848 but could not secure diplomatic recognition for Hungary. Sentenced to death *in absentia* after 1849 by the Austrians. Arrested by the police in Saxony in 1860 and extradited to the Austrians. Received amnesty on condition that he would not participate in politics. Invited to the Upper House after the October Diploma in 1860 where he opposed even *de facto* recognition of Francis Joseph as monarch. Committed suicide in 1861.

VASVÁRI, Pál (1826-1849). His father was a Greek orthodox priest and school principal. Attended private schools and the University of Budapest where he majored in history. Taught history in an exclusive progressive private school in Budapest before 1848. Another close friend of Petőfi's and an organizer of the March demonstration. Member of the Committee of Public Safety and a most important revolutionary agitator. Member of the Society for Equality. In October 1848 he led a group of volunteers against Jellačić. Later he was an officer in the revolutionary army. He was killed in action in 1849.

ZICHY, Count Ferenc (1811-1897). Conservative great estate owner. Presided over the Vice-Regency Council at Buda in the March Days. Opposed to the revolution. Served as Imperial administrator of a county occupied by the Austrians. Imperial High Commissioner attached to the Russian army operating in Hungary.

ZSEMBEREY, Imre (1804-1896). Gentry estate owner belonging to the liberal opposition before 1848. Became a radical deputy in the Assembly. Friend of József Madarász and member of Kossuth's revolutionary government after September 1848 but he was not an active participant.

## APPENDIX II
## CHRONOLOGY OF IMPORTANT EVENTS OF THE HUNGARIAN REVOLUTION OF 1848

*1847*

November 10 The last feudal Diet meets in Pozsony.

Early December University students in Budapest start debate on political questions.

*1848*

February 24 Revolution in Paris.

March 1 News of Paris revolution reaches Pozsony.

March 3 Kossuth delivers speech at Diet demanding abolition of feudalism and parliamentary government for Hungary and Habsburg Monarchy.

March 11 Formulation of popular demands called the Twelve Points by József Irinyi in Budapest.

March 13 Revolution in Vienna. Petőfi writes poem the "National Song."

Afternoon In Budapest the Opposition Circle discusses the Twelve Points and decides to circulate them before sending them to the Diet.

March 14 Morning News of Vienna revolution arrives Pozsony and the Diet accepts Kossuth's demands.

Afternoon In Budapest the Opposition Circle discusses the Twelve Points and decides to circulate them before sending them to the Diet.

Evening News of Vienna revolution arrives in Budapest.

March 15 Morning Revolutionary demonstration in Pest. Censorship is abolished.

Afternoon Popular meeting at City Hall. Formation of the Committee of Public Safety. Delegates from the Committee appear before the Vice-Regency Council. Táncsics released from prison.

Evening — Committee of Public Safety meets and takes over administration in Budapest. Celebration of victory at National Theatre.

March 15-16 — In Vienna Kossuth and a delegation from the Diet secure approval of national demands.

March 16 — Recruitment for National Guard begins in Budapest. Patriotic demonstrations.

March 17 — Batthyány appointed Prime Minister by the Palatine, Archduke Stephen. Rumors of peasant uprising.

March 18 — Diet passes bills concerning universal taxation, abolition of the tithe and feudal obligations of the peasantry.

March 19 — Archduke Stephen requests the King to veto bills of previous day. Delegation from the Committee of Public Safety presents Twelve Points to the Diet. Delegation sent from the Diet to the Committee. First issue of *March Fifteenth* published.

March 20 — Diet accepts a press law which abolished censhorship but makes large security downpayment prerequisite for the establishment of newspapers.

March 21 — Protest meeting in Budapest against press law. Establishment of a revolutionary committee for Pest county.

March 24 — Archduke Stephen recommends temporary accomodation with Batthyány in the interests of the dynasty.

March 26 — Committee of Public Safety demands "widest possible basis" for suffrage law.

March 27 — Popular meeting in Budapest demands royal approval

| | |
|---|---|
| | for separate Hungarian War and Finance Ministries. Proclamation of the Committee of Public Safety threatens dynasty with war if national demands are denied. |
| March 28 | Two royal communications to Diet reject independent War and Finance Ministries for Hungary and ask the Diet to discuss the bill liberating serfs again. |
| March 29 | Diet rejects royal communications. |
| March 29-31 | Mass demonstrations against the royal communications in Budapest. |
| March 31 | In a proclamation to the nation the Committee of Public Safety bids for national leadership. War and Finance Ministries granted and other national demands satisfied by Ferdinand. |
| April 1 | Ferdinand's capitulation becomes known in Budapest. Popular unrest decreases. |
| April 2 | First issue of *Workers' Newspaper* published. |
| April 11 | Ferdinand closes Diet in person and signs bills abolishing feudalism and making Hungary an independent parlimentary state. |
| April 14 | The Government moves from Pozsony to Budapest. |
| April 15 | Vasvári places the "power of the revolution" in the hands of the Cabinet. |
| April 15-May 8 | Withdrawal of the radicals. |
| April 19 | Anti-Semitic riots in Budapest. |
| April 20 | Government announces permits will be needed to hold popular meetings in Budapest. |

| | |
|---|---|
| May 8 | Establishment of the radical "March Club" in Budapest. |
| May 10 | Demonstration against Baron Lederer put down with military brutality. |
| May 11 | Popular meeting demands punishment of guilty soldiers and the radicals denounce Government. Radicalism on the rise in Budapest. |
| May 15 | Following new revolutionary demonstration in Vienna, the Court leaves for Innsbruck. |
| May 20 | Hungarian Government decides to invite Ferdinand to Budapest. |
| June 1 | First issue of *Radical Newspaper* published. |
| June 6 | Uprising by the Serbians starts in south Hungary. |
| June 10 | Batthyány promises military aid against the Italians to Vienna. Ferdinand suspends Jellačić from his office. |
| June 14 | Petőfi loses in the parliamentary election. |
| June 15-July 1 | Parliamentary elections. |
| July 5 | First meeting of the Representative Assembly. |
| July 6-12 | Conference of about 50 radical deputies attempts to formulate radical platform. |
| July 11 | Upon Kossuth's request, the Assembly unanimously votes for establishment of a Hungarian army of 200,000. |
| July 12 (?) | Establishment of the Society for Equality. |
| July 20-23 | Military aid to be used by Austrians against Italians violently denounced by the radicals in Assembly. |
| August 6 | Society for Equality demands emancipation of Jews. |

| | |
|---|---|
| August 13 | Political banquets are recommended in the Society for Equality. |
| August 14-19 | Debate over Army organization in Assembly. Increase in radical strength. Kossuth moves close to radicals' position. |
| August 15 | Talk about a second revolution in the Society for Equality. |
| August 16 | Petőfi writes of the possibility of second revolution in private letter. |
| August 23 | Society for Equality decides to hold great banquet on Sept. 8. Denunciation of Government intensifies. |
| August 27 | Cabinet agrees to the separation of Croatia from Hungary. |
| August 31 | Austrian Cabinet memorandum denies Hungary's right to independence. |
| Sept. 1 | *March Fifteenth* declares itself the "journal of revolutions and barricades." |
| Sept. 3 | Vasvári demands the dismissal of Cabinet and use of guillotine if necessary to save Hungary. The banquet is postponed. |
| Sept. 4 | Ferdinand reinstates Jellačić. |
| Sept. 5 | Large delegation from Assembly in Vienna asks Ferdinand to cease hostilities against Hungary. |
| Sept. 8 | The Society for Equality establishes permanent vigilante committee and decides to organize private army of 1,000. |
| Sept. 9 | Society for Equality withdraws decisions made previous day. |

| | |
|---|---|
| Sept. 10 | Batthyány Cabinet resigns. Cabinet crisis until September 28. |
| Sept. 11 | Jellačić invades Hungary. |
| Sept. 12 | Popular meeting organized by Society for Equality demands the appointment of Kossuth as Prime Minister. |
| Sept. 15 | Assembly abolishes the feudal dues on vineyards. |
| Sept. 16 | Establishment of the Committee of National Defense by the Assembly. Increased radical agitation. Cooperation between Kossuth and radicals. |
| Sept. 23 | Archduke Stephen resigns his office as Palatine and departs Hungary. |
| Sept. 25 | Ferdinand illegally appoints Lamberg Commander-in Chief of all armed forces in Hungary. |
| Sept. 27 | Assembly declares Lamberg's appointment null and void. |
| Sept. 28 | Lamberg murdered by excited mob in Budapest. Assembly temporarily entrusts executive power to the Committee of National Defense. |
| Sept. 29 | Jellačić defeated near Budapest. |
| October 1 | Jellačić begins withdrawal from Hungary. |
| October 3 | Ferdinand dissolves Assembly and names Jellačić temporary viceroy in Hungary. |
| October 4 | Four members of the Upper House added to the Committee of National Defense. |
| October 7 | Assembly declares Jellačić appointment null and void. |
| October 8 | Assembly gives executive power to Committee of National Defense permanently and makes Kossuth chairman. |

| | |
|---|---|
| December 2 | Ferdinand resigns and Francis Joseph ascends to throne. Not accepted in Hungary. |
| Dec.13-April 1, 1849 | Austrian offensive against Hungary. Retreat of Hungarian forces. |
| | *1849* |
| April-May | Victorious Hungarian counteroffensive. |
| April 14 | Dethronement of the House of Habsburg and declaration of Hungary's independence. |
| June 15-18 | Russian forces come to the aid of Austria. |
| August 13 | The main Hungarian army lays down arms at Világos. |

# NOTES

## CHAPTER I

1. Endre Arató, *A nemzetiségе kérdés története Magyarországon* [*History of the Nationality Question in Hungary*] (Budapest, Akadémiai Kiadó, 1961), I, 299.

2. These figures are based on a census taken in 1846 and should be treated with caution. The "Saxons" reffered to in the statistics were Germans in Transylvania. The "Others" were mostly Jews who became assimilated within one generation and spoke Magyar.

3. Endre Arató, Kálmán Benda, Gyula Mérei, György Spira, Zoltán Varga, *Magyarország története 1790-1849* [*History of Hungary, 1790-1849*] (Budapest, 1961), p. 127.

4. *Ibid.*, p. 151.

5. *Ibid.*, pp. 62-103, 123-56.

6. For Széchenyi and Kossuth see: Bálint Hóman and Gyula Szekfű, *Magyar történet* [*Hungarian History*] (Budapest, 1935-6), V, 257-74, 299-316, 339-43. Also, Sándor Szilágyi, ed., *A magyar nemzet története* [*History of the Hungarian Nation*] (Budapest, 1897), IX, 509-21, 539-64, 607-22.

7. Quoted by Mihály Horváth, *Huszonöt év Magyarország történelméből 1823-tól 1848-ig* [*Twenty-five Years from the History of Hungary from 1823 to 1848*] (Budapest, 1887), I, 186.

8. Dr. Dezső Márkus, ed., *1836-1868. évi törvenyczikkek* [*Law Articles Between 1836-1868*] (Budapest, 1896), p. 198.

9. Arató *et al.*, *op. cit.*, p. 227.

10. *Ibid.*, pp. 240, 266.

11. *Ibid.*, p. 276.

12. The complete text of the conservative program can be found in Horváth, *Huszonöt év, etc.*, III, 191-8.

13. István Barta, ed., *Kossuth Lajos az utolsó rendi országgyűlésen* [*L. Kossuth at the Last Feudal Diet*] (Budapest, 1951), pp. 152-7.

## CHAPTER II

1. Kálmán Benda, ed., *A magyar jakobinusok iratai* [*Writings of the Hungarian Jacobins*] (Budapest, 1957) I, 418-21. Martinovics wrote his autobiography for Emporer Leopold II in 1791.

2. Benda, ed., *op. cit.*, p. 1011. "Nobilis solus erit proprietarius."

3. *Ibid.*, pp. 1002-36. Texts of both catechisms.

4. *Ibid.*, p. lxxii. The total membership was estimated to be between 200-300.

5. József Madarász, *Emlékirataim* [*My Memoris*] (Budapest, 1883), p. 66.

6. *Ibid.*, p. 67.

7. Károly Berecz, *A régi "Fiatal Magyarország"* [*The Old "Young Hungary"*] (Budapest, 1898), p. 74.

8. Quoted by Dominic Kosáry, *A History of Hungary (Cleveland and New York, 1941), p. 203.*

9. Hóman and Szekfű, *op. cit.*, V, 298. Young radical intellectuals in the 1840's referred to themselves as Young Hungary. The term was used loosely. They had not formal organization.

10. Pál Pándi, ed., *A magyar irodalom története 1772-től-1849-ig* [*History of Hungarian Literature from 1772 to 1849*] (Budapest, 1965), p. 766.
Jókai recalled correctly. After Austrian troops occupied Budapest, Imperial authorities inventoried the possessions of known rebels preparatory to holding an auction. According to these records, Petőfi owned framed pictures of Roland, Kosciuszko, Desmoulins, Danton, Robespierre, St. Just, etc. Lajos Hatvany, *Igy élt Petőfi* [*Thus Lived Petőfi*] (Budapest, 1955-7), V, 153-4.

11. Mór Jókai, *Önmagáról* [*About Himself*] (Budapest, 1904), pp. 7-8.

12. Pál Pándi, ed, *Szöveggyüjtemény a forradalom és szabadsdgharc korának irodalmából* [*Anthology from the Literature of the Age of Revolution & War of Independence*] (Budapest, 1962) p. 315.

13. Sándor Petőfi, *Összes költeményei* [*Complete Poetry*] (Budapest, 1954), II, 188-9.

14. Sándor Fekete and József László, eds., *Vasvári Pál válogatott irásai* [*Selected Writings of P.V.*] (Budapest, 1954), pp. 127-8.

15. *Ibid.*, p. 129.

16. *Ibid.*, pp. 169-73.

17. *Ibid.*, pp. 137, 215.

18. *Ibid.*, pp. 199-206. These views appeared in a contemporary paper *Életképek* under the title "Michelet and the German Scientific System," in 1847.

19. The poem was first published on October 26, 1848 in the radcials' leading newspaper, *Marczius Tizenötödike* with the following note: "I wrote this poem in 1844; I do not need to explain why it was lying in the bottom of my desk until now."

20. Petőfi, *Összes költeményei*, pp. 639-40. "Egy gondolat bánt egemet" [I am Troubled by a Thought].

21. Sándor Petőfi, *Összes prózai művei és levelezése* [*Complete Prose and Correspondence*] (Budapest, 1960), p. 292.

22. *Ibid.*,p. 306. Letter written March 31, 1847.

23. Fekete and László, ed., *op. cit.*, pp. 219-22.

24. Petőfi, *Összes költeményei*, pp. 471-2.

25. *Ibid.*, II, 19-20. "A XIX század költöi" ("Poets of the Nineteenth Century").

26. Fekete and László, ed., *op. cit.*, p. 15.

27. László Geréb, ed., *Táncsics Mihály válogatott irásai* [*Selected Writings of M.T.*] (Budapest, 1954), pp. 129-33; 144-5.

28. *Ibid.*, p. 147.

29. Mihály Táncsics, *Életpályám* [*The Course of My Life*] (Budapest, 1949), p. 13.

## CHAPTER III

1. Pozsony is known as Pressburg in German and today it is called Bratislava. Since in the period discussed it was the constitutional center of Hungary, it seems appropriate to refer to it by its Hungarian name.

2. Barta, ed., *op. cit.*, pp. 425-7. Kossuth's letter to Wesselényi.

3. M. Horváth, *Huszonöt év,* III, 294-8. Also: György Spira, *A magyar forradalom 1848-49-ben.* [*The Hungarian Revolution in 1848-49*] (Budapest, 1959), pp. 63-7.

4. Menyhért Lónyai, 1847-48-diki naplója [Diary of M. Lónyai from 1847-8] (Budapest: Budapesti Szemle, 1896), I, 337-62.

6. Albert Nyári, *A magyar forradalom napjai* [*Days of the Hungarian Revolution*] (Pest, 1848), pp. 13-4.

7. Barta, ed., *op. cit.,* pp. 619-28.

8. R. John Rath, *The Viennese Revolution of 1848* (Austin, 1957), pp. 36, 62-3.

9. Dániel Irányi and Charles-Louis Chassin, *Histoire politique de la révolution de Hongrie 1847-49* (Paris 1859-60), II, 142. Irányi, a lawyer, was a member of the Opposition Circle and later a radical deputy and historian. Not to be confused with the journalist József Irinyi.

10. Jókai, *Életemből* [*From My Life*] (Budapest, 1898), I, 9. In an article entitled "The Youth of March."

11. Dénes Pap, ed ., *Okmánytár Magyarország függetlenségi harczának történetéhez* [*Collection of Documents to the History of Hungary's Independence War*] (Pest, 1868), I, pp. 12-3.

12. Rath, *op. cit.* p. 47. The exact form of universal representation was probably purposely left unclear.

13. Pap, ed., *Okmánytár.,* I, 15-6.

14. Spira, *op. cit.,* p. 75.

15. Petőfi, *Összes próza, etc.,* p. 405.

16. Alaios Degré, *Visszaemlékezéseim* [*My Recollections*] (Budapest, 1883), II, 4.

17. Petőfi, *Összes költeményei,* II, 367-8.

18. Degré, *op. cit,* II, 5-6. This description is supported by one of the typesetters of the Twelve Points. Hatvany, *op. cit.,*IV, 223-5.

19. Jókai, *Életemből,* I, 191.

20. Degré and Jókai differ on who it was. Degré says it was Petőfi and Jókai says it was Irinyi.

21. Ákos Birányi, *Pesti forradalom, martius 15-19* [*Revolution in Pest, March 15-19*] (Pest, 1848), p. 26.

22. Degré, *op. cit.,* II, 7.

23. Petőfi, *Összes próza, etc.,* p. 408.

24. Petőfi referred to it as the *Comité du salut public.*(*Ibid.,* p. 398-9.) The original name was *Pesti Rendfenntartási Bizottmány* which translated literally is the Committee for the Maintenance of Order in Pest. Pap, ed., *op. cit.,* I, 13-5.

25. Degré, *op. cit.,* II, 7.

26. Imre Deák, ed., *1848 A szabadsdgharc története levelekben, ahogyan a kortársak látták* [*1848 The History of the War of Independence in Letters as the Contemporaries Saw It*] (Budapest, 1942), pp. 27-8.

27. Petőfi, *Összes próza, etc.,* p. 502.

28. *Ibid.,* p. 409.

29. Arató *et al., op. cit.,* p. 151. This figure does not include the population of the suburbs and outskirts of the city. The total population was around 150,000. The revolutionaries later spoke "in the name of 160,000."

30. Jókai, *Életemből,* I, 97.

31. March 15 was the national holiday until the Communist takeover. Then it was replaced by April 4—the date of the "liberation" by the Red Army in 1945.

32. See description pp. 15.

33. Barta, ed., *op. cit.*, pp. 650-3.
34. Rath, *op. cit.*, pp. 87. 151.
35. Deák, ed., *op. cit.*, pp. 31-2. Letter of Archduke Palatine Stephen to Ferdinand V.
36. Pap, ed., *Okmánytár, etc.*, I, 20-2.
37. *Ibid.*, p. 19.
38. Deák, ed., *op. cit.*, p. 32. Personal letter to his secretary written March 17.

## CHAPTER IV

1. István Kléh, *A Pesti forradalom története, 1848-ban* [*History of the Revolution in Pest in 1848*] (Pest, 1848), pp. 29-33.
2. Biránvi, *op. cit.*, p. 56.
3. Kléh, *op. cit.*, pp. 36-7.
4. Petőfi, *Összes próza, etc.*, p. 398.
5. Degré, *op. cit.*, II, 10.
6. Deák, *op. cit.*, pp. 43-4.
7. *Ibid., p. 54.*
8. *Ibid.*, pp. 45-6.
9. Jókai, *Életemből*, I, 193.
10. *Márczius Tizenötödike,* (Budapest), March 19, 1848, p. 1.
11. Petőfi, *Összes költeményei*, II, 367.
12. *Marczius Tizenötödike,* March 20, 1848, p. 5.
13. Lónyai, *op. cit.*, II, 43.
14. Pap, ed., *Okmánytár*, I, 19-20. Circular dated March 17, 1848.
15. V. Eszter Waldapfel, ed., *A forradalom és szabadságharc levelestára* [*Collection of Letters from the Revolution and War of Independence*] (Budapest, 1950), I 150.
16. Hóman and Szekfű, *op. cit.*, V, 394.
17. Lónyai, *op. cit.*, II, 48. Another liberal aristocrat, Baron Podmaniczky, voiced the same fear of a peasant uprising. See Frigyes Podmaniczky, *Naplótöredékek* [*Parts of a Diary*] (Budapest, 1887) II, 230.
18. Deák, ed., *op. cit.*, p. 33. Letter to Court Chancellor László Szőgyény.
19. *Ibid.*, p. 49.
20. Jókai claimed that Széchenyi used Petőfi's poem in greeting his fellow "Glorious Great Lords" in the aristocrats' club in Pozsony before the Diet passed the legislation abolishing feudal obligations. According to Jókai, this action on Széchenyi's part was responsible for the lack of opposition on the conservatives' side. *Életemből*, II, 34-7. The story should not be accepted as evidence as Jókai was absent when this was reputed to have happened. But the gossip on which his stroy is based also contains the element of fear among the nobility.
21. Petőfi, *Összes próza, etc.*, p. 411.

## CHAPTER V

1. Biránvi, *op. cit.*, p. 29.
2. Pap, ed., *Okamánytár*, I, 13-4.

3. Kléh, *op. cit.*, pp. 29-30. Pap, ed., *Okmánytár, I, 14-5. Full text of the proclamations. They were publicized by the use of posters.*

4. *Pap, ed., Okmánytár,* I, 14-5.

5. Birányi, *op. cit.*, p. 36.

6. *Ibid.*, pp. 36, 46.

7. Spira, *op. cit.*, p. 88. Subsequent events showed the worthlessness of his word. When the arsenal was inspected by Hungarian government officials, 14,000 muskets and a like number of pistols were found. (*Marczius Tizenötödike),* May 11, 1848, pp. 194-5.

8. Degré, *op. cit.*, II, 10-1.

9. *Ibid.*, p. 35.

10. The capital originally consisted of two units, Buda and Pest, separated by the Danube. In 1848 Buda still had a separate municipal council.

11. Birányi, *Op. cit.*, p. 51.

12. Priscilla Robertson, *Revolutions of 1848: A Social History* (New York, 1960), pp. 338-9.

*13.* Birányi, *op. cit.*, p. 54.

14. *Ibid.*, p. 51.

15. *Ibid.*, p. 46.

16. Petőfi, *Összes próza,* pp. 410-1.

17. Birányi, *op. cit.*, p. 46.

18. *Ibid.*, pp. 36, 38-9.

19. *Ibid.*, p. 46.

20. *Ibid.*, p. 46.

21. Bulyovszky, *Naplótöredék* in Hatvany, *op. cit.*, IV, 269-71. Bulyovszky recounted that Vasvári had lost his voice from talking too much and this may be why Hajnik, was the spokesman. Hajnik later became police chief in Budapest.

22. Barta, ed., *op. cit.*, p. 674.

23. *Ibid.*, p. 675.

24. *Emlékkönyv Kossuth Lajos születésének 150 évfordulójára* [*Testimonial to the 150th Anniversary of the Birth of Louis Kossuth*] (Budapest, 1952), II, 150.

25. *Marczius Tizenötödike,* March 21, 1848, p. 9.

26. *Ibid.*, p. 11-2.

27. The delegation members from the Upper House considered the mission a "dangerous journey." One of them , Baron Podmaniczky, wrote that even wives estranged for their husbands came to the harbor to see them off on the steamship leaving for the capital. Frigyes Podmaniczky, *Naplótöredékek* [*Fractions of a Diary*] (Budapest, 1897), II, 234-5.

28. Detailed descriptions of the scene appeared in the newspapers. Pap, Okmánytár, etc., I, 25-7. The correctness of the reporting is proved by the fact that the essence of the delegation's assurance corresponds to a Diet resolution of the same day also promising a new representative assembly upon completion of the most urgent legislation. Barta, ed., *op. cit.*, pp. 668-9.

29. Pap, *Okmánytár, etc.*, I, 27.

30. Spira, *op. cit.*, p. 106.

31. *Marczius Tizenötödike,* March 22, 1848, p. 16.

32. *Ibid.*, p. 16.

33. Revolutionary students in Vienna also successfully opposed a restrictive press law there on April 1. Rath, *op. cit.*, pp. 131-2.

34. Podmaniczky, *op. cit.*, II, 228.

35. Between March 16 and April 1, 60 cities and counties contacted the Committee of Public Safety. The list is contained in Szilágyi, ed., *op. cit.*, X 41.

36. Marczius Tizenötödike, March 21, 1848, p. 12.

37. The city of Pest originally had its own municipal organization which the Committee took over. The county of Pest was the administrative district around the capital with a separate central building and bureaucracy.

38. Barta, *op. cit.*, pp. 682-4. The minutes and description of the meeting are given in *March Fifteenth,* March 21, 1848, pp. 10-1.

39. *Ibid.*, p. 686.

40. *Ibid.*, pp. 685-6.

41. *Ibid.*, pp. 685-6.

42. Spira, *op. cit.*, p. 108.

43. *Marczius Tizenötödike,* March 24, 1848, p. 22.

44. Pap, ed., *Okamdnytdr, etc.*, I, 27-8. Letter of appointment dated March 23, 1848.

45. Ferenc Pulszky, who also claimed to be a member of the provisional ministerial group, stated in his memoris that the Committee was not dissolved because they had need of it. The situation was such, however, that the ministerial group did not have the power to do so. Pulszky admits that they had only "moral power." Ferenc Pulszky, *Életem és korom* [*My Life and Times*] (Budapest, 1884), I, 296-9.

## CHAPTER VI

1. Deák, ed., *op. cit.*, pp. 45-6. Full text.

2. Deák, ed., *op. cit.*, p. 33.

3. Márkus, ed., *op. cit.*, p. 223. See more detailed description of the electoral law in this paper on page 60.

4. Detailed account of the meeting in *Marczius Tizenötödike,* March 27, 1848, pp. 37-8.

5. The term "proletarian" was widely used among the 1848 radicals. They did not necessarily mean a member of the industrial working class. They applied the term to include poor people in general.

6. *Marczius Tizenötödike,* March 28, 1848, p. 28.

7. Pap, ed., *Okmdnytár, etc.*, I, 35-40. Full text of both documents.

8. Partial text. Description of the meeting and the full text of the proclamation in *Marczius Tizenötödike,* March 28, 1848, p. 41 and also Pap, ed., *Okmánytár, etc.*, I, 33-4.

9. *Marczius Tizenötödike,* March 28, 1848, p. 42.

10. *Ibid.*, p. 42.

11. Deák, ed., *op. cit.*, p. 54. Zichy to Vice-Chancellor Szögyény-Marich on March 29, 1848.

12. Petőfi, *Összes költeményei,* pp. 375-7. According to Szekfű, Petőfi read the poem at a popular meeting on March 27. Hóman and Szekfű, *op. cit.*, V, 393. It seems certain that the poem was written between March 27-30. It was printed in leaflet form on April 1.

13. Birányi, *op. cit.*, p. 61.

14. Pap, ed., *Okmánytár, etc.*, I, 39.

15. *Ibid.*, p. 39.

16. Barta, ed., *op. cit.*, pp. 701-2.

17. Pap,ed., *Okmánytár, etc.*, I, 42-4.
18. *Marczius Tizenötödike,* March 31, 1848, p. 52.
19. Degré, *op. cit.*, II, 15.
20. Birányi, *op. cit.*, p. 61.
21. The composition of this group or the purpose of flying the red flag are not known. Red feathers and red flags symbolized revolutionary defiance in Hungary in 1848.
22. *Marczius Tizenötödike,* March 31, 1848, p. 52.
23. Birányi, *op. cit.*, p. 61.
24. Pulszky, *op. cit.*, p. 298.
25. Pap, ed., *Okmánytár, etc.*, I, 46.
26. *Ibid.*, I, 44-5.
27. Degré, *op. cit.*, II, 14. The "youth" in contemporary usage meant the young revolutionaries.
28. Pap, *Okmánytár, etc.*, I, 44-5.
29. Barta, ed., *op. cit.*, pp. 706-10.
30. *Marczius Tizenötödike,* April 1, 1848, p. 56.
31. Petőfi, *Összes próza, etc.*, p. 412.
32. Horváth, ed., *Huszonöt év, etc.*, III, 501-4.
33. Fekete and László, ed., *op. cit.*, pp. 286-8.
34. Full text of the April Laws in Márkus, ed., *op. cit.*, pp. 215-55. English summary in William Stiles, *Austria in 1848-49* (New York, 1852), II, 375-9.

## CHAPTER VII

1. Fekete and László, eds., *op. cit.*, p. 299.
2. Hatvany, *op. cit.*, IV, 371, 389-91.
3. *Ibid.*, pp. 344-5.
4. Hatvany, *op. cit.*, III, 346.
5. Fekete and László, eds., *op. cit.*, p. 301.
6. *Marczius Tizenötödike,* May 1, 1848, p. 159; May 9, 1848, p. 187.
7. *Ibid.*, April 19, 1848, p. 120.
8. See this paper pages 29-30
9. *Ibid.*, April 20, 1848, p. 123.
10. Pap, ed., *Okmánytár, etc.*, I, 57-9.
11. *Marczius Tizenötödike,* April 20, 1848, p. 133.
12. *Ibid.*, April 22, 1848, p. 132.
13. Fekete, *op. cit.*, p. 28.
14. Petőfi, *Összes költeményei,* II, 570-2.
15. Fekete and László, eds., *op. cit.*, pp. 290-1.
16. *Ibid.*, pp. 290-1.
17. Petőfi also expressed similar sentiments; *Összes próza, etc.*, p. 412.
18. Fekete and László, eds., *op. cit.*, pp. 288-91. Full text of speech.
19. Photocopy of the poster is published in Spira, *op. cit.*, p. 184.
20. Degré, *op. cit.*, II, 11-2.
21. Spira, *op. cit.*, pp. 182-92.
22. Fekete and László, eds., *op. cit.*, p. 71.
23. Statistics from Spira, *op. cit.*, p. 136.
24. Spira, *op. cit.*, pp. 139-41.

25. Georges Lefebvre, *The Coming of the French Revolution* (New York, 1960), p. 120. In describing the burdens of the French peasantry before the revolution, mention is made of hunting and fishing rights, the right to maintain mills, ovens or wine presses and market tolls as among the exclusive privileges of the nobility.

26. A detailed county-by-county account of the peasant unrest has been collected by Győző Ember, ed., *Iratok az 1848-i magyarországi parasztmozgalmak történetéhez* [*Documents to the History of Peasant Movements in Hungary in 1848*] (Budapest, 1959), p. 280. See pp. 21, 25, 27, 29, 39, 41 for use of army against peasants.

27. Fekete and László, eds., *op. cit.*, pp. 295-8.

28. Quoted in *Kossuth Emlékkönyv, etc.*, II, 170.

29. Fekete, *op. cit.*, p. 108. Spira, *op. cit.*, p. 178.

30. Mihály Táncsics, *Életpályám* [*The Course of My Life*] (Budapest, 1949), p. 243.

31. *Munkások Ujsága,* April 16, 1848, pp. 36-8.

32. *Ibid.*, July 16, 1848, p. 243.

33. *Ibid.*, July 2, 1848, pp. 224-7.

34. *Ibid.*, May 7, 1848, pp. 88-91; April 23, 1848, p. 52.

35. Táncsics, *op. cit.*, p. 248.

36. *Munkások Ujsága,* April 2, 1848, pp. 11-3.

37. Táncsics, *op. cit.*, p. 244.

## CHAPTER VIII

1. *Marczius Tizenötödike,* April 13, 1848, p. 99.
2. *Ibid.*, May 9, 1848, p. 186.
3. *Ibid.*, April 18, 1848, p. 116.
4. *Ibid.*, April 24, 1848, p. 135.
5. *Ibid.*, April 25, 1848, p. 138.
6. *Ibid.*, May 6, 1848, p. 178.
7. *Ibid.*, May 6, 1848, p. 178.
8. *Ibid.*, May 9, 1848, p. 186.
9. Pap, ed., *Okmánytár, etc.*, I, 77. Royal order to Colonel Mészáros.
10. The King's letter to Archduke Stephen on Hungary's share in the Imperial state debt appeared in both the Viennese and Hungarian papers. Full text by Pap, *Okmánytár, etc.*, I, 48-9. Kossuth estimated the total state revenue at 28 million. Other sources putit at 34.2 million. Barta, ed., *op. cit.*, p. 707.
11. *Marczius Tizenötödike,* April 16, 1848, p. 109.
12. The term "party" was used loosely by the radicals. It did not have the meaning of present-day usage.
13. *Marczius Tizenötödike,* April 17, 1848, p. 111.
14. *Ibid.*, May 6, 1848, p. 178.
15. *Munkások Ujsága,* May 7, 1848, p. 86.
16. *Marczius Tizenötödike,* May 9, 1848, pp. 188-9. Full text of the charter.

## CHAPTER IX

1, Account by a special investigation commission appointed by the Cabinet, including interviews with numerous witnesses from among the civilians and military. Pap, ed., *etc.*, I, 93-107. *Marczius Tizenötödike*, May 11, 1848, pp. 194-5.

2. *Marczius Tizenötödike*, May 11, 1848, p. 194. (Front page).

3. Petőfi, *Összes próza, etc.*, p. 460.

4. *Munkások Ujsága*, May 21, 1848, pp. 115-6.

5. Degré, *op. cit.*, II, 26-7. See also Táncsics, *op. cit.*, p. 250. There is no account of the membership or activities of the second delegation which went to Archduke Stephen.

6. See page 55 of this paper.

7. István Sinkovics, ed., *Kossuth Lajos az első magyar felelős minisztériumban* [*L. Kossuth in the First Responsible Hungarian Cabinet*] (Budapest, 1957), pp. 153-4.

8. *Marczius Tizenötödike*, May 19, 1848, pp. 225-6. June 2, 1848, p. 271 and June 10, 1848, p. 300.

9. *Ibid.*, May 19, 1848, p. 226.

10. 300 forints were the equivalent to about U.S. $150 at that time according to the American Chargé d'Affaires. Stiles, *op. cit.*, II, 55.

11. Horváth, *Huszonöt év, etc.*, III, 399.

12. *Marczius Tizenötödike*, May 25, 1848, p. 244.

13. *Ibid.*, June 8, 1848. p. 291.

14. *Ibid.*, May 20, 1848, p. 228.

15. Petőfi, *Összes próza, etc.*, pp. 425-6.

16. *Ibid.*, p. 426.

17. *Marczius Tizenötödike*, June 21, 1848, p. 336.

18. Robertson, *op. cit.*, p. 233.

19. Sinkovics, ed., *op. cit.*, p. 153-4.

20. *Ibid.*, p. 237.

21. *Munkások Ujsága*, June 4, 1848, p. 147.

22. Summary of Irányi's platform is found in *Marczius Tizenötödike*, June 29, 1848, p. 365; and July 3, 1848, p. 376-7.

23. *Ibid.*, July 5, 1848, p. 385.

24. Petőfi, *Összes próza, etc.*, p. 429.

25. From a statement signed by 176 electors protesting the irregularities at the election, addressed to the Minister of Justice. *Ibid.*, p. 431-2.

26. Dénes Pap, ed., *A magyar nemzetgyülés Pesten 1848-ban* [*The Hungarian National Assembly in Pest in 1848*] (Budapest, 1881), I, 26-47. For the verification of the mandate of Petőfi's opponent, an Assembly investigating commission was named. Because many of Petőfi's supporters had left to join the National Guard, the investigation was postponed and actually never materialized. See Zoltán Ferenczi, *Petőfi életrajza* [*Biography of Petőfi*] (Budapest, 1896), III, 257.

27. Beér, ed., *op. cit.*, p. 15.

28. *Ibid.*, p. 17.

## CHAPTER X

1. Dr. Árpád Károlyi, *Németujvári Gróf Batthyány Lajos első magyar miniszterelnök főbenjáró pöre* [*The High Treason Trial of the First Hungarian Prime Minister, Count Louis Batthyány of Németujvár*] (Budapest, 1932), II, 611. Original document reprinted from the Viennese State Archives, Kolowrat, Anton: "Die erledigte Banus-Stelle muss durch einen kräftigen, populären Mann besetzt . . . Bei der hohen Dringlichkeit des Gegenstandes unterlege ich den Vorschlag, ohne weiteres die Person zu bezeichnen, welcher die wichtige militärische und zivile Macht des Banus anvertraut werden könnte. Der Name des Obristen des Ersten Banal-Gränz-Infanterie-Regimentes *Joseph Freiherrn von Jellachich dürfte für sich schon ein Gegengewicht gegen das treiben der Ultra-Magyaren sein. a)* Am 20. März 1848. Fr. Gr. Kolowrat, mp."

2. *Ibid.*, pp. 610-1.

3. Pap, ed., *Okmánytár, etc.*, I, 265-6.

4. Many of the various nationality groups in Hungary held meetings of their own attended by their leaders.

5. Address of the Serbian National Meeting gathered at Karlovicz to His Majesty, June 10, 1848. Pap, ed., *Okmánytár, etc.*, I, 179-81.

6. Minutes of the Transylvanian Rumanian Nation's National Meeting held in Balázsfalva. *Ibid.*, I, 115-22.

7. Quoted by Spira, *op. cit.*, pp. 166-7.

Point 1. "The Slovak people do not wish to oppress other nations, but will not allow themselves to be oppressed either."

Point 2. "A general parliament of all brother nations living in Hungary should be organized."

Point 3. "The nations [of Hungary] should have their own national legislatures . . ."

Point 14. "The Slovak nation expresses its respect toward the Hungarian Government and sends greetings to all those Hungarian citizens who support its claims."

8. Speech given at the Diet, April 8. Barta, ed., *op. cit .*, p. 732.

9. Pap, ed., *Okmánytár, etc.*, I, 254-7.

10. Royal Manifesto to the Croatians and Slavonians. *Ibid.*, pp. 186-92.

11. After Jellačić's dismissal by the king, he led a delegation to Innsbruck and before the whole Court he demanded the separation of the Triune Kingdom from Hungary and its attachment to Austria. He recommended that the monarch regain his supremacy over the Magyars with the help of the Slavs. See M. Hartley, *The Man Who Saved Austria* (London, 1912), p. 179.

12. Pulszky, *op. cit .*, II, 330-2.

13. Károlyi, *op. cit.*, II, 628-9. Minutes of the Cabinet meeting.

14. Pap, ed., *Okmánytár, etc.*, I, 47.

15. *Marczius Tizenötödike,* April 19, 1848, p. 119,

16. *Ibid.*, August 15, 1848, p. 526.

17. Horváth, *Huszonöt év, etc.*, III, 475.

18. *Marczius Tizenötödike,* June 8, 1848, p. 292.

19. *Ibid.*, June 15, 1848. p. 314.

20. *Ibid.*, May 26, 1848, p. 248.

21. *Ibid.*, July 8, 1848, p. 397.

22. *Ibid.*, June 3, 1848, p. 275.

23. Petőfi, *Összes költeményei,* II, 568-70.

24. *Munkások Ujsága,* July 16, 1848, p. 240.

25. In September the radicals called for terror not only against the insurgent nationalities but counterrevolutionary Magyars as well. Terror was not used on a large scale in either case. About 7,500 men of Jellačić's invading army, after their capture by the Hungarians, were allowed to return to Croatia unharmed. Their officers were treated as prisoners of war and received regular pay from the Hungarian Government.

## CHAPTER XI

1. The royal communiqué giving plenipotentiary powers to Archduke Stephen was read to the first Assembly meeting. Pap, ed., *Nemzetgyülés Pesten* [*The National Assembly in Pest*] (Budapest, 1881), I, 5-7.
2. *Ibid.,* pp. 7-10.
3. Hóman and Szekfű, *op. cit.,* V, 499.
4. Pap, ed., *Nemzetgyülés Pesten,* I, 12.
5. *Munkások Ujsága,* July 16, 1848, p. 244.
6. Táncsics, *op. cit.,* p. 253.
7. Report of J.A. Blackwell to the British Ambassador in Vienna on the important figures of the 1844 Hungarian Diet. Zoltán Horváth, *Teleki László* (Budapest, 1964), II, 117.
8. J. Madarász, *op. cit.,* pp. 122-4.
9. *Ibid.,* p. 244 and p. 134 and Táncsics, *op. cit.,* pp. 252-4.
10. *Munkások Ujsága,* July 23, 1848, pp. 260-1.
11. The first issue of the *Radical Lap* appeared on June 1, 1848.
12. *Radical Lap,* (Budapest), July 5, 1848, p. 105.
13. *Ibid.,* July 9, 1848, p. 112.
14. Quoted by Fekete, *op. cit.,* pp. 114-5.
15. The name "Society for Equality" reminds one of Babeuf's organization in France in the 1790's. It is almost certain that the name of the Hungarian radical club was borrowed from the "Society of Equals." However, to the Hungarian radicals, equality meant only equality of rights. They did not even lean toward equality of means which was the most important feature of Babeuf's program.
16. The name *Népelem Radical Lap* translated literally would be *Democracy Radical Newspaper.* The name *Radical Democrat* is considered a closer rendition into meaningful English. On August 8 it was merged with another opposition paper, the *Reform.* The title of the paper was not changed, however.
17. Pap, ed., *Nemzetgyülés Pesten,* I, 24.
18. *Ibid.,* p. 26.
19. *Ibid.,* p. 54.
20. *Ibid.,* pp. 54-61. Speeches of the radical deputies.
21. *Ibid.,* pp. 73-88. See also, Madarász, *op. cit.,* pp. 136-7.

## CHAPTER XII

1. Robertson, *op. cit.,* p. 353.

2. "Ungarici fratres! Agitur de communi redemptione in libertate nostra: et proprium periculum quaerit, qui contra fratrem pugnat... Sic iterum Italia et Ungaria inter nationes vocate, in osculum pacis et cinculo fraternitatis junctae, invincibiles forent ab inimicis gloriae et libertatis eorum. Ungarici! Quid vobis profecit pugnare ad defensionem Mariae Theresiae? Gratitudo Austriae? Dilegium et servitudo! Frangite jugum et surgite!" Pap, ed., *Okmánytár, etc.,* I, 48.

3. Pap, ed., *Nemzetgyülés Pesten,* I, 135-52.

4. *Ibid.,* p. 153. The Pragmatic Sanction, ratified by the Hungarian Diet in 1723, accepted the succession of the female line of the House of Habsburg in Hungary and promised to aid the ruling house against foreign aggression. Full text: Stiles, *op. cit.,* II, 369-71.

5. Fekete and László, eds., *op. cit.,* pp. 283-7.

6. Pap, ed., *Nemzetgyülés Pesten,* I, 155-9.

7. *Marczius Tizenötödike,* July 19, 1848, p. 431.

8. *Ibid.,* July 20, 1848, p. 435.

9. *Népelem Radical Lap,* July 22, 1848, p. 73; July 23, 1848, p. 80.

10. *Munkások Ujsága,* July 30, 1848, p. 275.

11. Pap, ed., *Nemzetgyülés Pesten,* I, 182-7.

12. *Ibid.,* I, 182-7.

13. *Ibid.,* I, 191.

14. *Marczius Tizenötödike,* July 26, 1848, p. 459.

15. *Ibid.,* July 24, 1848, p. 441.

16. Pap, ed., *Nemzetgyülés Pesten,* I, 212, 256-7.

17. *Ibid,* I, 210-1.

18. *Ibid.,* I, 259.

19. *Ibid.,* I, 245-6.

20. *Ibid.,* I, 267.

## CHAPTER XIII

1. Perczel charged them with treason in the Assembly. Even General Mészáros, who had always been very loyal to his fellow officers, noted in his memoirs that the commander of the Hungarian forces in the south, Bechtold, deployed his troops in such a way that nothing could come of his encounters. Quoted by Spira, *op. cit.,* p. 227.

2. Beér, *op. cit.,* p. 53. Batthyány explained his views in a closed session of the Assembl

3. Spira, *op. cit.,* p. 223.

4. Beér, ed., *op. cit.,* pp. 561-2. Text of proposed army bill.

5. Pap, ed., *Nemzetgyülés Pesten,* I, 393-9.

6. *Marczius Tizenötödike,* July 28, 1848, p. 466; August 23, 1848, p. 553.

7. Pap, ed., *Nemzetgyülés Pesten,* I, 388-90.

8. *Ibid.,* I, p. 387-439; II, 1-40.

9. *Ibid.,* I, 419-26.

10. *Ibid.,* I, 402.

11. Pap, ed,. *Nemzetgyülés Pesten,* II, 33.

12. *Marczius Tizenötödike,* August 22, 1848, p. 449.

13. Pap, ed., *Nemzetgyülés Pesten,* I, 428-36.

14. Sinkovics, ed., *op. cit.,* p. 642.

15. *Marczius Tizenötödike,* May 25, 1848, p. 243.
16. *Ibid.,* June 30, 1848, p. 368.
17. *Ibid.,* July 31, 1848, p. 474.
18. *Ibid.,* August 4, 1848, p. 490.
19. Petőfi, *Összes költeményei,* II, 402-3.
20. *Ibid.,* II, 403-5.
21. *Ibid.,* II, 445-6.
22. *Ibid.,* II, 413-5.
23. The *March Fifteenth* sadly commented that the situation in the capital had changed since March because the young men who had made the revolution had left to give their lives and blood for their country. September 6, 1848, p. 631.
24. *Kossuth Emlékkönyv, etc.,* II, 191.
25. See page 78 in this paper.
26. *Radical Lap,* June 3, 1848, p. 9; June 29, p. 89; July 6, p. 109; etc.
27. Beér, ed., *op. cit.,* p. 669. The bill was never debated.
28. *Népelem Radical Lap,* August 2, 1848, pp. 111-2. The paper, as the official organ of the Society, gave detailed accounts of each meeting and printed the texts of all resolutions. It is the main source for information on the Society's activities which, insofar as is known, have not been examined by any historian nor commented on apart from passing remarks. Note: The word "capitalists" is a literal translation from Hungarian: "tőpénzes."
29. *Ibid.,* August 8, 1848, p. 130. Text of the resolution. Further description of the discussion on Jewish emancipation, *Ibid.,* August 10, 1848, p. 139.
30. Beér, ed., *op. cit.,* p. 869-70.
31. *Ibid.,* p. 873. Full text of the law.
32. For bills proposed by radical deputies see Beér, ed., *op. cit.,* pp. 636-40.
33. *Ibid.,* p. 685. Pap, ed., *Nemzetgyülés Pesten,* II, 232.
34. *Népelem Radical Lap,* August 18, 1848, p. 162.
35. *Ibid.,* August 21, 1848, p. 174.
36. *Ibid.,* August 29, 1848, p. 199.
37. *Ibid.,* August 24, 1848, p. 183.
38. Petőfi, *Összes próza, etc.,* pp. 463-4. Letter to János Arany dated August 16, 1848. Nation").
39. Petőfi, *Összes próza, etc.,* pp. 463-4. Letter to János Arnay dated August 16, 1848.
40. Petőfi, *Összes költémenyei,* II, 455-6.

## CHAPTER XIV

*The question of a second revolution in September 1848 is one of the least examined aspects of the 1848 revolution in Hungary. Most Hungarian historians pass over the possibility with a few non-committal sentences. The greatest nineteenth century historian of the revolutionary period, Mihály Horváth, in a three-volume work merely mentions that the radicals of the Society for Equality made heated speeches against the machinations of the reactionaries and had the audacity to form a vigilante committee in September and the organization was dissolved by the police. Horváth, *op. cit.,* I, 357-9. The best twentieth century Hungarian historian, Gyula Szekfű, referred to the radicals in

September in four lines to the effect that the radicals spread French-type revolutionary propaganda and that the Madarász brothers were preparing lists of proscription. Hóman and Szekfű, *op. cit.*, V. 415. Even the Marxist György Spira never states that preparations were made for a second revolution. Spira, *op. cit.*, pp. 243-5. The reasons for this sketchy treatment may be the lack of massive documentary evidence on the one hand, and a lack of a detailed study of the newspaper of the Society for Equality, on the other hand. It is quite possible that those survivors of the revolution who were among the leading members of the Society purposely did not deal with its activities in their memoirs to any great extent because of a feeling of patriotic piety. Since even the moderate Batthyány was executed by the Austrians after the revolution and became a martyr for freedom, it seems reasonable to conjecture that no one wished to talk about revolutionary plots against his government after his death.

1. *Népelem Radical Lap,* August 31, 1848, p. 207.

2. Lajos Kovács, "A szeptemberi napok 1848-ban" ("The September Days in 1848"), *Budapesti Szemle* [*Budapest Review*], XXXV (1883), 264.

3. *Marczius Tizenötödike,* September 1, 1848, p. 585.

4. Waldepel, ed., *op. cit.*, I, 399.

5. ". . . unser Angst ist, das die Sache nicht mehr lange dauern kan, die innere Verwaltung des Landes kostet in 7 Monaten mehr als unser Oesterreich in 5 Jahren, man macht kein Geheimnis mehr daraus, das am 7ten September bey Gelegenheit eines Banquets an welchen 15,000 Baueren Theil nehmen werden, die Ministers ausser Kossuth u. Szemere zum abdanken gezwungen werden. Die Sache wird ernst werden, obgleich wir nichts an Truppen haben als ein schwaches Grenadier Battaillon u. 400 Man von Tursky Inf.: Zichy major. Ofen, am 31 August." *Ibid.*, I, 407. (Note that Zichy mistook the date to be September 7.)

6. Deák, ed., *op. cit.*, pp. 211-3.

7. An account of the meeting which Topler described also appeared in their newspaper which confirms the substance of Topler's report. *Népelem Radical Lap,* September 6, 1848, pp. 227-8.

8. Fekete, *op. cit.*, p. 176.

9. Pap, ed., *Nemzetgyülés Pesten,* II, 148-9.

10. *Népelem Radical Lap,* September 6, 1848, p. 228.

11. Pap, ed., *Okmánytár, etc.*, I, 403-18.

12. *Ibid.*, I, 401-2.

13. The very moderate Deák described the futility of the mission in an embittered letter dated September 5. Károlyi, *op. cit.*, II, 9-11.

14. See page 69 in this paper.

15. Deák, ed., *op. cit.*, p. 211.

16. Pap, ed., *Nemzetgyülés Pesten,* II, 157.

17. *Ibid.*, II, 164-6. Pázmándy read the full text of his speech to the Assembly after the delegation had returned to Budapest.

18. Viscount Ponsonby to Viscount Palmerston, *Correspondence Relative to the Affairs in Hungary, 1847-49* (London, 1850), p. 82.

19. *Marczius Tizenötödike,* September 5, 1848, p. 598.

20. *Népelem Radical Lap,* September 7, 1848, p. 229.

21 *Ibid.*, September 10, 1848, pp. 241-2.

22. József Madarász, for instance, a key figure in the Society for Equality, wrote in

depth about the revolution in his memoirs, but does not even mention the formation of the vigilante committee or the planned private army. Rather than giving any information about the Society, he chose to write only about generally known developments taking place in the Assembly during the September days.

23. Kovács, *op. cit.*, XXXV, 263.

24. Károlyi, *op. cit.*, II, 7-9. Letter to Archduke Francis Charles.

25. *Ibid.*, pp. 11-2. Letter dated Sept. 6, 1848 from Archduke Francis Charles to Archduke Stephen.

26. Kossuth published the account of this conversation in 1881 on the basis of his notes from 1850. Sinkovics, ed., *op. cit.*, II, 929-30.

27. Károlyi, *op. cit.*,I, 116-7. Kossuth and the radical Irányi protested in the Assembly Sept. 13 the presence of these troops.

28. Horváth, *Magyarország, etc.*, I, 355.

29. *Népelem Radical Lap,* September 10, 1848, p. 244.

30. Pap, ed., *Nemzetgyülés Pesten,* II, 180-2, 195-7.

31. *Ibid.*, pp. 254-5.

32. Hartley, *op. cit.*, pp. 214-5.

33. Beér, ed., *op. cit.*, p. 232.

34. Pap. ed., *Nemzetgyülés, Pesten,* II, 247-9.

35. *Ibid.*, pp. 283-5. Deák's account of his mission imcluded the written communication of the Imperial Parliament to him.

36. *Correspondence Relative to the Affairs of Hungary*, p. 83.

37. Pap, ed., *Nemzetgyülés Pesten,* II, 233.

38. Deák, ed., *op. cit.*, pp. 219-20. Ferdinand's letter to Archduke Stephen.

39. A private letter of one of Jellačić's army officers is revealing about the behavior of his troops. "They can't be kept from excesses and they rob and steal frightfully. We order a thousand floggings to be administered every day, but it is of no use. Not even a God, much less an officer, could hold them back. We receive kind treatment from the peasants but every evening come complaints, sometimes dreadful ones. I am driven to desparation by this robber-train and feel no better than a brigand myself." Hartley, *op. cit.*, p. 232.

40. *Marczius Tizenötödike,* September 11, 1848, p. 617.

41. *Népelem Radical Lap,* September 15, 1848, p. 258.

42. Sinkovics, ed., *op. cit.*, pp. 921-2.

43. Pap, ed., *Nemzetgyülés Pesten,* II, 204.

44. *Ibid.*, pp. 208-9.

45. *Ibid.*, p. 238.

46. *Marczius Tizenötödike,* September 13, 1848, p. 627.

47. *Népelem Radical Lap,* September 13, 1848, p. 257.

48. Pap, ed., *Nemzetgyülés Pesten,* II, 195.

49. *Ibid.*, pp. 21-2.

50. Kovács, *op. cit.*, XXXV, 263.

51. Horváth, *Magyarország függetlenségi, etc.*, I, 382.

52. *Népelem Radical Lap,* September 12, 1848, p. 247.

53. Text of his proclamation appeared in the official newspaper *Közlöny* [*Communications*], Budapest, September 15, 1848, p. 497.

54. Spira, *op. cit.*, p. 254.

55. *Munkások Ujsága,* September 14, 1848, p. 388.

56. Petőfi's proclamation appeared in *Népelem Radical Lap,* September 20, 1848, pp. 273-4 and *Munkások Ujsága,* September 24, 1848, pp. 409-11.

57. This guerilla warfare had far-reaching consequences. Among the captured mail was a personal letter from Jellačić to Latour, the Imperial War Minister, proving Latour's active support of Jellačić. The letter was read to the Assembly in Budapest and its contents became known in Vienna also. It was a major factor in creating the anger against Latour which cost him his life on October 6, 1848.

58. Kossuth's suggestions and Batthyány's response in Pap, ed., *Nemzetgyülés Pesten,* II, 242-4.

59. J. Madarász, *op. cit.,* pp. 169-70.

60. Pap, ed., *Nemzetgyülés Pesten,* II, 281-2.

61. *Ibid.,* pp. 282, 289.

62. Spira, *op. cit.,* p. 270.

63. Jókai, *Önmagáról,* p. 147.

64. Spira, *op. cit.,* p. 270.

65. Pap, ed., *Nemzetgyülés Pesten,* II, 305.

66. *Marczius Tizenötödike,* September 19, 1848, p. 646.

67. Pap, ed., *Okmánytár, etc.,* II, 78-9.

68. Text of the manifestoes, *Ibid.,* pp. 39-44.

69. Márkus, ed., *op. cit.,* p. 218.

70. Pap, ed., *NemzetgyülésPesten,* II, 303-10.

71. Waldapfel, ed., *op. cit.,* II, 129.

72. *Marczius Tizenötödike,* September 29, 1848, p. 681.

73. Pap,ed., *Okmánytár, etc.,* II, 102-3.

74. Pap, ed., *Nemzetgyülés Pesten,* II, 312.

75. Petőfi, *Összes költeményei,* II, 592-4.

76. Beér, ed., *op. cit.,* p. 255.

77. *Közlöny,* October 9, 1848, p. 609; October 10, 1848, p. 613.

78. Pap, ed., *Nemzetgyülés Pesten,* II, 344. The enlargement of the Committe occurred on October 4, five days after Jellačić's defeat at Pákozd.

79. *Ibid.,* pp. 344-5.

80. Pap, ed., *Nemzetgyülés Pesten,* II, 364-5. Full text read to the Assembly on October 7.

81. *Ibid.,* pp, 377-80.

82. Beér, ed., *op. cit.,* p. 273.

## CHAPTER XV

1. *Marczius Tizenötödike,* Sept. 30, 1848, pp. 685-6; Oct. 9, 1848, p. 710; Oct. 11, 1848, p. 717; Oct. 14, 1848, p. 731; Oct. 24, 1848, pp. 764-5, etc.

2. Károly Kornis, *A kormány rendszerről szózat a néphez* [*Manifesto to the People about the System of Government*] (Vacz, 1848), 24 pp. The second pamphlet with the same title was published in Budapest, 1848, 31 pp.

3. Kornis, *op. cit.,* II, 16.

4. Ákos Birányi, *Köztársasági káté* [*Republican Catechism*] (Pest, 1848), p. 5.

5. *Ibid.,* pp. 26-32.

6. Pap, ed., *Okmánytár, etc.* II, 261-3.

7. A.J.P. Taylor, *The Habsburg Monarchy 1809-1918* (New York, 1965), p. 81. *See also:* Szilagyi, ed., *op. cit.,* X, 268-88.

8. Complete text of the Declaration of Independence, Beér, ed., *op. cit.*, pp. 721-53. A somewhat inaccurate English translation is in Stiles, *op. cit.*, II, 409-19.

9. Dénes Pap, ed., *A parlament Debrecenben* [*The Parliament in Debrecen*] (Lipcse, 1870), II, 60-88.

10. *Ibid.*,I, 28.

11. Jókai's newspaper in Debrecen, *Esti Lapok* [*Evening Newspaper*], became the organ of the Peace Party.

12. Táncsics, *op. cit.*, p. 265.

13. Hóman and Szekfű, *op. cit.*, V, 432.

# BIBLIOGRAPHY

*Note:* Since most of the sources quoted in the paper were written in Hungarian, English translations of the titles and descriptive notes were added in the bibliography.

All translations in the text and bibliography were made by the author. Poems were translated without attempting to render them into English poetry.

## A. PRIMARY SOURCES

Andics, Erzsébet. (ed.). *A nagybirtokos arisztokrácia ellenforradalmi szerepe 1848-49-ben. (The Counterrevolutionary Role of the Great Estate Owner Aristocracy in 1848-49.).* 2 vols. Budapest: Akadémiai Kiadó, 1952-65.
Collection of documents from 1848-49. Includes private correspondence of aristocrats as well as official documents from Windischgrätz, Schwarzenberg, Francis Joseph, etc. All documents published in the original language. Many in German, some in French.

Austrian State Archives. Vienna: Kabinetts Archiv, Geheime Acten Karton #10 and Karton #12.
General information about revolutionary Hungary. Nothing specific about the radicals.

Barta, István. (ed.). *Kossuth Lajos az országos honvédelmi bizottmány élén. (L. Kossuth at the Head of the National Committee of Defense).* 2 vols. Budapest: Akadémiai Kiadó, 1952-3.
Speeches, letters, articles, official papers of Kossuth. Vol. 1, Sept.-Dec. 1848. Vol. 2, Jan.-April. 1849.

----. *Kossuth Lajos az utolsó rendi országgyülésen. (L. Kossuth at the Last Diet of the Estates).* Budapest: Akadémiai Kiadó, 1951.
Speeches and writings of Kossuth at the end of 1847 and before April 1848.

----. *Kossuth Lajos kormányzóelnöki iratai. (Writings of L. Kossuth During His Governing-Presidency).* Budapest: Akadémiai Kiadó, 1955. 974 pp.
Covers April-August, 1849.

Beér, János. (ed.). *As 1848/49 évi népképviseleti országgyülés. ( The 1848/49 Popular Representative Assembly).* Budapest: Akadémiai Kiadó, 1954. 933pp.
The text of the minutes of every parliamentary session. Rules, proposed bills, laws and resolutions passed by the Assembly in 1848-49. Together with the parliamentary diaries edited by Pap, (see below), the complete account of all parliamentary activities.

Benda, Kálmán. (ed.). *A magyar jakobinusok iratai. (Writings of the Hungarian Jacobins).* Budapest: Akadémiai Kiadó, 1952-57. 3 vols.
Collection of documents about the Martinovics conspiracy. Some of the material is in German and Latin.

Berecz, Károly. *A régi "Fiatal Magyarország". (The Old "Young Hungary").* Budapest: Athenaeum, 1898. 192 pp.
Berecz was a journalist and member of the literati circle of Petőfi. His memoirs contain interesting stories about the everyday affairs of important historic figures.

Birányi, Ákos. *Köztársasági káté. (Republican Catechism).* Pest: Magyar Mihály, 1848. 48pp.
Revolutionary pamphlet advocating the republican form of government.

-----. *Pesti forradalom (martius 15-19). (Revolution in Pest, March 15-19).* Pest: Magyar Mihály, 1848. 63 pp.
Detailed account of the four days of the revolution based on the minutes of the Committee of Public Safety as well as the author's first-hand impressions. Since the original minutes of the Committee were lost, this pamphlet remains as the best source for the history of the first four days of the revolution in the capital.

Bóka, László, (ed.). *Gróf Széchenyi István naplói. (Diaries of Count I. Széchenyi).* Budapest: Ardói, n.d. 362 pp.
Selections from the diary of Count Széchenyi.

Boros, Mihály. *Politikai kis káté a nép számára. ( A Little Political Catechism for the People).* Budapest: Emich Gusztáv, 1848. 16 pp.
Pamphlet explaining the meaning of legal equality and the April Laws; intended for the peasantry.

*Correspondence Relative to the Affairs of Hungary 1847-49. Presented to both Houses of Parliament by Command of Her Majesty. August 15, 1850.* London: Harrison & Son.
English diplomatic dispatches to Lord Palmerston from Vienna. In general hostile to Hungary.

Deák, Imre. (ed.). *1848: A szabadságharc története levelekben, ahogyan a kortársak látták. ( 1848: The History of the War of Independence in Letters, as the Contemporaries Saw It)* Budapest: Sirály Könyvkiadó, 1942. 431 pp.
Collection of private letters and official correspondence of King Ferdinand, the Palatine and other important political figures.

*Debreczeni Lapok.* (*Debrecen Newspaper*). Debrecen, 1849. A radical paper edited by the Madarász brothers. Irregular. Issued in March and April 1849.

Degré, Alajos. *Visszaemlékezéseim.* (*My Recollections*). Budapest: Pfeifer Ferdinand Kiadása, 1883. 2 vols. Memoirs of one of the leading figures of the revolution. Valuable.

Ember, Győző. (ed.). *Iratok as 1848-i magyarországi parasztmozgalmak töténetéhez.* (*Documents to the History of the 1848 Peasant Movements in Hungary*). Budapest: Közoktatásügyi Kiadóvállalat, 1959. 280 pp.
Collection of documents illustrating peasant unrest in Hungary in 1848.

Fekete, Sándor and László, József. (ed.). *Vasvári Pál válogatott irásai.*(*Selected Writings of P. Vasvári).* Budapest: Művelt Nép Könyvkiadó, 1956. 312 pp.
The most complete edition of Vasvári's essays and speeches.

Gereb, László. (ed.). *Táncsics Mihály válogatott irásai.* (*Selected Writings of M. Táncsics*). Budapest: Táncsics Könyvkiadó, 1954. 526 pp.

Hatvany, Lajos. *Igy élt Petőfi.* (*Thus Lived Petőfi*). Budapest: Akadémiai Kiadó, 1955-57. 5 vols.
Contains thousands of pages of recollections of Petőfi's contemporaries as well as the author's own, somewhat confused account of Petőfi's life. Was used as a primary source.

Jókai, Mór. *Életemből.* (*From My Life*). Budapest: Révai Testvérek, 1898. 2 vols.
Collection of Jókai's autobiographical articles.

——. *Önmagáról.* (*About Himself*). Budapest: Franklin Társulat, 1904. 384 pp.
Collection of Jókai's autobiographical articles.

Kazinczy, Gábor. "Szerepem a forradalomban" ("My Role in the Revolution"). Article in *Hazánk*, 1884. pp. 84-105. The self-defense of a moderate deputy before the Austrian military tribunal in 1850. Indicts the *March Fifteenth,* the radicals and Kossuth for the revolution.

Kemény, G. Gábor. (ed.). *Teleki László válogatott munkái.* (*Selected Works of L. Teleki*). Budapest: Szépirodalmi Könyvkiadó, 1961. 2 vols.
Literary and political writings of a radical aristocrat.

Klapka, General György. *Memoirs of the War of Independence in Hungary.* London: Charles Gilpin, 1850. 2 vols.
Personal recollections of an important military leader of the revolution. Primarily about military affairs but includes historical introduction and important documents in the appendix. 2 vols. (II, 203-334).

Kléh, István. *A pesti forradalom története 1848-ban.* (*History of the Revolution in Pest in 1848.*). Pest: Magyar Mihály, 1848. 42 pp.
Pamphlet written March 1848 giving an eyewitness account of the revolution in Budapest.

Kornis, Károly. *A kormány rendszerről szózat a néphez.* (*Manifesto to the People about the System of Government*). Vácz: Somogy, 1848. 24 pp.
A " second volume" was published with the same title. Budapest: Eisenfels, 1848, 31 pp. Pamphlets. Arguments by a law professor for the republican form of government.

*Kossuth Lajos 1848-49-ben.* (*L. Kossuth in 1848-49*). Budapest: Akadémiai Kiadó, 1951-57. 5 vols.
See under editors of individual volumes (Barta, Sinkovics).

Kovács, Lajos. "A szeptemberi napok 1848-ban" ("The September Days in 1848"), *Budapesti Szemle* (*Budapest Review*), XXXV (1883), 65-85; 251-279; 349-385. XXXVI (1883), 60-81.
Historical essay by an ignorant and intellectually dishonest opponent of the revolution. He was a deputy in 1848 and some of his personal observations add to the general picture.

*Közlöny.* (*Communications*). Budapest, 1848-49.

The official newspaper of the Government. Daily. Printed all decrees, orders, promotions, etc. and also the Assembly diaries. Some issues were published in Debrecen in 1849.

*Köztársasági Lapok*. (*Republican Newspaper*). Budapest, 1848. Weekly. Only a few issues appeared in October and November 1848. It did not print news but rather theorectical arguments for the republican form of government.

"Lónyai Menyhért 1847-8-diki naplója" ("The 1847-8 Diary of M. Lónyai"), *Budapesti Szemle* (*Budapest Review*). I (1896), 337-62. II (1896), 18-49.
Diary of a political opponent of Kossuth. Describes conditions from the viewpoint of the moderately liberal gentry.

Madarász, József. *Emlékirataim*. (*My Memoirs*). Budapest: Franklin Társulat, 1883. 528 pp.
Valuable contribution from a radical gentry deputy.

*Marczius Tizenötödike*. (*March Fifteenth*). Budapest, 1848-49.
Daily of the radical intellectual In 1849 some issues were published in Debrecen.

Márkus, Dezső. (ed.). *1836-1868 évi törvényczikkek*. (*Law Articles 1836-1868*). Budapest: Franklin Társulat, 1896. 600 pp.
Full texts of all laws between 1836-68. The volume carries the inscription Corpus Juris Hungarici.

*Munkások Ujsága*.(*Workers' Newspaper*). Budapest, 1848.
Appeared twice weekly. Most articles written by the editor Táncsics for the peasantry.

*Népelem*. (*Democracy*). Budapest, 1848.
Radical daily edited by the Madarász brothers. Only a few issues appeared in June and July 1848. Merged with *Radical Lap* (*Radical Newspaper*) on July 16.

*Népelem Radical Lap*. (*Radical Democrat*). Budapest, 1848.
Started from merger of two separate papers *(Népelem* and *Radical Lap).* Translated literally would be *Democracy Radical Newspaper*. Became the official organ of the Society for Equality under the direction Madarász brothers.

Nyári, Albert. *A magyar forradalom napjai. (Days of the Hungarian Revolution).* Pest: Magyar Mihály, 1848.
Pamphlet written by young radical intellectual;incomplete, the author never finished it.

Pap, Dénes. (ed.). *A magyar nemzetgyülés Pesten 1848-ban*. (*The Hungarian National Assembly in Pest in 1848*). Budapest: Ráth Mór, 1881. 2 vols.
Parliamentary diary containing all speeches and proceedings but not the resolutions or minutes.

------. *A parlament Debrecenben*. (*The Parliament in Debrecen*). Lipcse: Köhler K.A., 1870. 2 vols.
Parliamentary diary containing all speeches and proceedings of 1849 Debrecen parliament but not the resolutions or minutes.

——. *Okmánytár Magyarország függetlenségi harczának történetéhez 1848-49.* (*Collection of Documents to the War of Independence of Hungary, 1848-1849*). Pest: Heckenast Gusztáv, 1868-69. 2 vols.
Extremely important documentary evidence covering all aspects of the revolution.

Pándi, Pál. (ed.). *Szöveggyüjtemény a forradalom és szabadságharc korának irodalmából.* (*Anthology from the Literature of the Age of Revolution and Independence War*). Budapest: Tankönyvkiadó, 1962.
Selections primarily from writers and poets from 1848-49.

Petőfi, Sándor. *Összes költeményei.* (*Complete Poetry*). Budapest: Szépirodalmi Könyvkiadó, 1954. 2 vols.

——. *Összes prózai művei és levelezése.* (*Complete Prose Works and Correspondence*). Budapest: Szépirodalmi Könyvkiadó, 1960. 757 pp.

Podmanicky, Frigyes. *Naplótöredékek.* (*Fractions of a Diary). Budapest: Grill Károly, 1887. 4 vols.*
*Podmaniczky was a liberal aristocrat and member of the Upper House.* Vol. 2 of his diary contains much information about the revolutionary period.

Pulszky, Ferenc. *Életem és korom. (My Life and Times).* Budapest: Franklin Társulat, 1884. 2 vols.
Pulszky was the Undersecretary for Foreign Affairs in the Batthyány Cabinet and held other improtant positions. His memoirs provide valuable information otherwise unavailable on the revolution.

*Radical Lap.* (Radical Newspaper). Budapest, 1848.
Radical daily edited by M. Mérei between June 1-July 16, 1848. It merged with *Népelem* on July 16, 1848.

Sinkovics, István. (ed.). *Kossuth Lajos az első magyar felelős miniszteriumban.* (*L. Kossuth in the First Responsible Hungarian Cabinet*). Budapest: Akadémiai Kiadó, 1957. 1,098 pp.
Speeches, articles, official papers of Kossuth while in Batthyány Cabinet. Covers April-September 1848.

Táncsics, Mihály. *Életpályám. (The Course of My Life).* Budapest: Révai Könyvkiadó, 1949, 463 pp.
Autobiography of a radical revolutionary.

Tordai, György. (ed.). *Forradalom és a papi rend.* (*Revolution and the Ecclesiastic Estate*). Budapest: Kossuth Könyvkiadó, 1961. 182 pp.
Selections from anticlerical articles of the newspapers in the revolutionary period.

Waldapfel, V. Eszter, (ed.). *A forradalom és szabadságharc levelestára.* (*Collection of Letters of the Revolution and War of Independence).* Budapest: Közoktatásügyi Kiadó-Gondolat, 1950-65. 4 vols.
Collection of private and official letters from 1848-49. High government officials, politicians and simple people are represented. A kind of public opinion survey from the revolutionary period.

Zerffi, Gusztáv. *Martius 15-dike 1848 Pesten.* (*March 15, 1848 in Pest*). Pest: Hartleben, 1848. 38 pp.
Pamphlet describing the events of March 15.

B. SECONDARY SOURCES

Acsádi, Ignác. *A magyar jobbágyság története. (History of Hungarian Serfdom).* Budapest: Grill Károly Könyvkiadóvállalata, 1908. 551 pp.
Excellent survey of the development of the institution of serfdom from the establishment of the Hungarian state until 1848.

Arató, Endre. *A nemzetiségi kérdés története Magyarországon.* (*History of the Nationality Question in Hungary*). Budapest: Akadémiai Kiadó, 1960. 2 vols.

Arató, Endre; Benda, Kálmán; Mérei, Gyula; Spira, György and Varga, Zoltán. *Magyarország története 1790-1849.* (*History of Hungary 1790-1849*). Budapest: Tankönyvkiadó, 1961. 584 pp.
The most recent general history of the period written by the best living historians in Hungary.

Bodolay, Géza. *Irodalmi diáktársaságok 1785-1848.* (*Literary Student Associations 1785-1848*). Budapest: Akadémiai Kiadó, 1963. 810 pp.
Detailed examination of literary student associations in Hungary. Important information about the formative years of revolutionary figures.

Dezsényi, Béla. "A magyar hirlapirodalom 1848-49" ("The Hungarian Press in 1848-49"), *Irodalomtörténet,* (1949), pp. 105-116.

Ember, Győző. (ed.). *Az 1848/49-i miniszterium levéltára.* (*Archives of the 1848/49 Cabinet*). Budapest: Akadémiai Kiadó, 1950. 279 pp.
Guide to the archives of the 1848-49 Cabinet.

*Emlékkönyv Kossuth Lajos születésének 150 évfordulójára.*(*Testimonial Volume to the 150th Anniversary of the Birth of L. Kossuth*). Budapest: Akadémiai Kiadó, 1952. 2 vols.
Essays about various aspects of Kossuth's political career.

Fekete, Sándor. *A márciusi fiatalok.* (*The Youth of March*). Budapest: Szikra, 1950. 245 pp.
Study of the radical intellectuals in 1848. Strong Marxist bias and numerous factual errors.

Fejtő, Francois. (ed.). *The Opening of an Era. 1848. An Historical Symposium.* New York: Howard Fertig, 1966. 444 pp.

Ferenczi, Zoltán. *Petőfi életrajza.* (*Biography of Petőfi*). Budapest: Franklin Társulat, 1896. 3 vols.
Scholarly biography with primary emphasis on the details of the poet's life rather than on esthetic analysis of his poetry.

Gracza, György. *Az 1848-49 iki magyar szabadságharc története.* (*History of the 1848-49 Hungarian War of Independence).* Budapest: Lampel Könyvkiadó, 1894-98. 5 vols.
Out-of-date popular history with numerous factual errors.

Grünwald, Béla. *A régi Magyarország 1711-1825.* (*The Old Hungary 1711-1825*). Budapest: Franklin Társulat, 1888. 576 pp.
Excellent political and social history.

------. *Az új Magyarország: gróf Széchenyi István.* (*The New Hungary: Count I. Széchenyi*). Budapest : Franklin Társulat, 1888. 529 pp.
Scholarly biography of Széchenyi.

Hartely, M. *The Man Who Saved Austria. The Life and Times of Baron Jellačić.* London: Mills & Boon Ltd., 1912. 372 pp.
Unscholarly biography trying to present Jellačić as a "German soldier" and a Croat national hero at the same time. Numerous factual errors.

*Hóman, Bálint and Szekfű, Gyula. Magyar történet.* (*Hungarian History*). Budapest: KirályiMagyar Egyetemi Nyomda, 1935-36. 5 vols.
The best twentieth century history of the Hungarian people. Vol. 5, the work of Szekfű, covers the revolutionary period.

Horváth, Mihály. *Huszonöt év Magyarország történelméből 1823- tól 1848-ig.* (*Twenty-five Years from the History of Hungary Between 1823-1848*). Pest: Ráth Mór, 1887. 3 vols.
Still the best account of the period.

------. *Magyarország függetlenségi harcának története 1848 és 1849-ben.* (*History of Hungary's War of Independence in 1848 and 1849*). Pest: Ráth Mór, 1871-72. 3 vols.
The best nineteenth century scholarly account of 1848-49.

Horváth, Zoltán. *Teleki László 1810-1861.* Budapest: Akadémiai Kiadó, 1964. 2 vols.
Vol. 1, Scholarly biography of the radical Teleki. Vol. 2, Collection of documents about his life.

Irányi, Dániel and Chassin, Charles-Louis. *Historie politique de la revolution de Hongrie, 1847-1849.* Paris: Pagnerre, 1859-60. 2 vols.
A good account of the revolution by a member of the radical left. Pro-revolutionary viewpoint.

Jakab, Elek. *Szabadságharczunk történetéhez. Visszaemlékezések 1848-49-re.* (*History of Our War of Independence. Recollections from 1848-49).* Budapest: Aigner Lajos, 1881. 577 pp.
History of Transylvania in 1848-49 based in part on personal recollections of the author.

Kann, Robert A. *The Habsburg Empire. A Study in Integration and Disintegration.* New York: Frederick A. Praeger, 1957. 227 pp.

Károlyi, Árpád. *Németújvári gróf Batthyány Lajos első magyar miniszterelnök főbenjáró pöre.* (*High Treason Trial of the First Hungarian Prime Minister, Count L. Batthyány of Németújvár*). Budapest: Magyar Történelmi Társulat, 1932. 2 vols. Vol. 1, Description of Batthyány's trial and the analysis of political issues raised during the trial. Vol. 2, Collection of documents pertinent to 1848.

------. *Az 1848-diki pozsonyi törvénycikkek az udvar előtt.* (*The 1848 Laws of Pozsony Before the Court*). Budapest: Magyar Történelmi Társulat, 1936. 374 pp.
Detailed examination of the proceedings of the State Council in Vienna in regard to the April Laws. Contains 152 pages of documents from the Vienna State Archives.

Király, István; Pándi, Pál and Sőtér, István. *A magyar irodalom története 1849-1905.* (*History of Hungarian Literature 1849-1905*). Budapest: Gondolat, 1963. 492 pp.

Kosáry, Dominic G. *A History of Hungary.* Cleveland, New York: The Benjamin Franklin Bibliophile Society, 1941. 482 pp.

------. "Perczel Mór feljegyzései" ("Notes of Mór Perczel") *Századok* (*Centuries*), LXXI (1937), 304-22.
Description of the autobiographical notes of a radical deputy and general.

Macartney, C.A. *A Short History of Hungary.* Chicago: Aldine Publishing Co., 1962. 262 pp.

Mód, Aladár. *400 év küzdelem az önálló Magyarországért.* (*400 Year Struggle for an Independent Hungary*). Budapest: Szikra, 1954. 743 pp.
General survey of Hungarian history. Marxist.

Pándi, Pál. (ed.). *A magyar irodalom története 1772-től 1849-ig.* (*History of Hungarian Literature from 1772 to 1849*). Budapest: Akadémiai Kiadó, 1965. 831 pp.

Pándi, Pál and Tóth, Dezső. *Tanulmányok Petőfiről.* (*Essays about Petőfi*). Budapest: Akadémiai Kiadó, 1962. 509 pp.
Essays primarily on the esthetic aspects of Petőfi's poetry.

Rath, R. John. *The Viennese Revolution of 1848.* Austin: University of Texas Press, 1957. 424 pp.

Robertson, Priscilla. *Revolutions of 1848: A Social History.* New York: Harper & Bros., 1960. 464 pp.

Spira, György. *A magyar forradalom 1848-49-ben.* (*The Hungarian Revolution in 1848-49*). Budapest: Gondolat, 1959. 676 pp.
Best modern account covering 1848-49 revolution. Marxist.

Stiles, W.H. *Austria in 1848-49.* New York: Harper & Bros. Publishers, 1852. 2 vols.
An account by the U.S. Chargé d'Affaires in Vienna of the revolutions in the Habsburg Empire. Devotes much space to Hungary.

Supka, Géza. *1848: A márciusi forradalom előzményei, lefolyása, társadalmi jelentősége.* (*1848: The Antecedents, Course and Social Significance of the March Revolution*). Budapest: Cserépfalvi, 1938 (?). 297 pp.
Somewhat journalistic account of the revolution during the spring and summer of 1848. Written from the viewpoint of a radical democrat.

Szabó, Ervin. *Társadalmi és pártharcok a 48-49-es magyar forradalomban.* (*Social and Party Struggles in the 48-49 Hungarian Revolution*). Vienna: Bécsi Magyar Kiadó, 1921. 383 pp.
Ultra-Marxist, sectarian, looking only for elements of the class struggle in 1848.

Szemere, Bartholomew de. *Hungary from 1848 to 1860.* London: Richard Benley, 1860. 269 pp.
Szemere was Minister of Interior in 1848. This volume was written in letter form to Richard Cobden, M.P. Information for sympathetic Englishman about the issues of the Hungarian revolution.

Szilágyi, Sándor. *A magyar forradalom férfiai 1848-49-ből.* (*Men of the Hungarian Revolution from 1848-49*). Pest: Heckenast Gusztáv, 1850. 344 pp.
Biographies of the leading participants of the revolution.

——. (ed.). *A magyar nemzet története.* (*History of the Hungarian Nation*). Budapest: Athenaeum, 1895-98. 10 vols.
A history of Hungary from the earliest times. Vol. 9 discusses the period 1815-47 and Vol. 10 the period thereafter up to the 1890's.

Taylor, A.J.P. *The Habsburg Monarchy 1809-1819.* New York: Harper & Row. Publishers, 1965. 279 pp.

Tordai, György. *Az 1848-as márciusi ifjak az egyházról és a vallásról. (The Youth of March 1848 about the Church and Religion*). Budapest: Kossuth Könyvkiadó, 1965. 264 pp.
Study of the anticlericalism of the revolutionary radical intellectuals in 1848.

## INDEX